I FLEW
INTO
TROUBLE

I FLEW INTO TROUBLE

Story of a WWII Navigator

Patricia Calder

IGUANA

Copyright © 2024 Patricia Calder
Published by Iguana Books
720 Bathurst Street
Toronto, ON M5S 2R4

All rights reserved. No part of this publication may be reproduced, stored in a retrieval system or transmitted, in any form or by any means, electronic, mechanical, recording or otherwise (except brief passages for purposes of review) without the prior permission of the author.

Publisher: Cheryl Hawley
Proofreader: Lee Parpart
Front cover design: Jonathan Relph

ISBN 978-1-77180-699-2 (paperback)
ISBN 978-1-77180-698-5 (epub)

This is an original print edition of *I Flew into Trouble*.

To my grandmother, Mary Agnes Calder, who collected the documents that form the backbone of Jack's story, who stood up for me and inspired me, and who sat beside me as a ghost writer. Without her, this book would not have been possible.

To all the veterans and families who lived through those days.

To my parents, who endured and bore their grief in silence.

Introduction

My grandmother's scrapbook fell into my possession by surprise, a gift from a cousin. I considered it a treasure but it took me ten years to unlock the secrets it holds.

My uncle, Jack Calder J4695, served as an RAF (Royal Air Force) navigator from 1940–1944. My grandmother collected every letter, telegram, and newspaper clipping following his career.

Before the war Jack Calder had been a reporter and editor for Canadian Press, logging sports stories from around Ontario and Quebec. He covered the Montreal hockey riot where he met and remained lifelong friends with McGill footballer Bobby Keefer.

Because Jack was already well known before the war, colleagues plastered his picture beside every story covering the stages of the Commonwealth Air Training Plan, and even followed the beginning of his life in the UK.

But Jack wasn't content with other reporters writing about him; he wanted to write from his own perspective, that of an RAF navigator.

Grandmother's scrapbook is a jumble of over 100 items pasted at random as the mailman delivered one story at a time of Jack into her hands. When I first laid eyes on the contents I didn't know what I had inherited. I didn't know Uncle Jack. I only knew that Grandmother had saved his story, and that she wanted it remembered.

My first task was to open the contents of the scrapbook, all the letters that no one had seen in more than seventy-five years, with their permanent creases so fragile I was afraid to flatten them. I needed to photograph every item in order to sort them chronologically, digitize the whole and therein discover Jack's story.

The veterans are dying and their stories are dying with them. That's why I wrote this book — to share Jack's story so that Grandmother's efforts to preserve his legacy would not be in vain.

This is Jack's story. Ralph Keefer's book *Grounded in Eire*, 2001, tells another version of Jack's story. I have dipped and dived into Keefer's book multiple times, with permission, at times paraphrasing and at other times quoting verbatim from his account of my uncle's experiences in the war.

Other sources also document parts of Jack's life. The University of Windsor website, *Jack Calder at War,* takes the viewer through my grandmother's scrapbook of WWII. Heidi Jacobs has written extensively on Jack's pre-war journalism career. The Chatham-Kent Sports Network features "Jack Calder Was a Man with a Story," written by Scott Chandler. Scott also published a comic book using Jack's voice as narrator. All of these tidbits about my mother's famous brother fell into my hands while I was preparing to write Jack's story.

Dear Reader, make no mistake: this book is a work of fiction, but it is seriously grounded in fact. Jack Calder was a historically significant person recognized by two universities, two national museums (the Irish and Canadian War Museums), three books, two websites and a comic book.

Only two original letters from Jack survive, but his voice is also heard in all the newspaper articles he wrote. I began to imagine other letters he might have written, along with ones he might have received, and I sat down to tell his story.

Part One

1940–41

Dear Mom,   Nov. 22, 1940

I'm turning my back on Air Observer School and Alberta, leaving for Toronto tomorrow so I plan to be home for one more Christmas before shipping out. If we are all together, do you think you could arrange to have a family portrait taken? I'd like to have a touchstone in my breast pocket while I'm flying.

My report card indicates that my prospects of becoming a pilot are dim: "a very nervous pilot not recommended for service flying." However, I have "above average ability" as a navigator. The report states that Calder is "quiet and steady, respected by fellows and a natural leader; reliable, not excitable; a fine type, cool." The navigator is the one who plots the route to and from the target, so I will have the responsibility of calculating it accurately by a system called dead reckoning. With pencil I will use charts, compass, watch, and protractor, add variations for weather, and watch the ground for rivers, railways, and roads to read our way. Of course, cloud cover will complicate things. The crew will be relying on me so there will be pressure besides what the barometer reads.

I hope I will be brave when the minutes and seconds count, but I won't know until I'm tested. I'm concerned that a single minute could be critical — life or death. Oh Mom, once I see action, I'm sure I'll be fine.

Of course, I hope one of your goals will be writing to me and my brothers. I'll try to do my part from across the pond.

In January my whole class will be presented with wings in a ceremony at Jarvis in Toronto. Then we'll board trains for Montreal, Quebec City, and ultimately Halifax and the troop boat. It's pretty exciting for a boy from small town Ontario to have the chance to travel, even into the teeth of war. I'm full of energy and anticipation now but I do wonder what's ahead and how I will measure up to my own expectations. Most of the boys I talk to are smiling, but I see uncertainty in their eyes. I'm not alone in these feelings but we don't talk about them. We don't want to seem unpatriotic. We've had lectures about the importance of maintaining high morale.

Thanks for being a great listener, Mom. You have remarkable intuitive radar. You understand why we have to join, don't you? I remember in my teens no matter how late I turned up you would always be waiting, ready to chat, open to hear anything at all that was on my mind. It's comforting to know that you will be home late at night with a cup of tea or a dram of Irish whiskey same as always when the rain is falling and I'm full of questions. Love, *Jack*

Dear Mom and Dad,   **Jan. 2, 1941**

We arrived safely in the UK surrounded by a thick mist in the gray chilly dawn. Our spirits were high as we sang "Roll out the Barrel," "We're Here Because We're Here," and "O Canada" and tramped onto the pier. The low-hanging fog concealed seaplanes droning an overhead salute, and we could hear drums rolling a greeting. A few men, women and children of the seaside village came pouring out of their homes, but otherwise our arrival was a secret affair. However, Anthony Eden, Secretary of State for the Dominions, and Vincent Massey, Canadian high commissioner in London, were present to welcome us. Eden's speech was printed in the paper so I'm copying it for you to hear how noble our purpose is:

> A nation of the new world is offering its help to challenge tyranny in the old. Your example is a guarantee of final victory, but it has been more than that. It is an inspiration to freedom-loving peoples everywhere.... You were convoyed across the Atlantic by the warships of the French navy, acting in close co-operation with His Majesty's ships.... Every arrangement in this important and difficult operation has been made in almost complete secrecy and carried out with equal success.

The mayor of the port, who could not disclose the name of his town, said, "You have come here ... on a crusade of peace and enforcement of international law and to aid in the struggle against dictatorship.... We know this struggle will end in final victory for Allied arms."

During the Atlantic crossing our convoy was closely guarded by French and British warships. The closest thing to a scare occurred on the second wintry day away from home shores when a submarine-shaped hulk loomed ahead. The surge of excitement passed quickly when it turned out to be a whale — and a dead whale at that. Machine guns poked their snouts skyward from the upper decks of our ship, augmenting a four-inch gun in the stern. All were manned around the clock — the machine guns by steel-helmeted soldiers, the four-incher by the British naval rifle crew.

All of us were compelled to wear lifebelts night and day during the crossing, plus we had periodic lifeboat drills. Between "Reveille" and "Lights Out" were boxing and wrestling contests, movies and sing-songs each night, organized by representatives of Canadian Legion War Services, the YMCA, and Sally Ann. The entertainment was certainly a distraction.

On the ship with us were artillery from Winnipeg and Montreal, engineers from Toronto and Halifax, signal units, ambulance units and infantry including several kilted Scotch regiments accompanied by their own pipe band.

Even before the UK was made aware of our arrival, we had been disembarked, cordially greeted in a brief ceremony at the quayside and whisked off to Aldershot.

Let the last leg of our training begin. We are excited to look into the eyes of the enemy and stare down his fear. I love you both. *Jack*

Dear Jack,   Jan. 15, 1941

I graduated from nursing. Yay! Mother came to the ceremony but Dad didn't. I suppose he still hasn't forgiven me for running away and leaving them without help at home. Someone gave me a dozen red roses. I know it wasn't Dad. Was it you? It must have been. Thank you so much. All the other girls had bouquets so I wasn't left out. A professional photographer took pictures and I'll send you one when they are printed. The roses were the most gorgeous colour, magenta, almost as deep red as a garnet, my birthstone. The fragrance was heavenly. I dried the petals.

Do you know that rose petals retain their fragrance forever? That's what nosegays are made from. I'm going to save mine for my lingerie drawer. Too much information?

When I ran away from home and hitchhiked to London, the sisters of St. Joseph were kind enough to accept me into the nursing program without Mom and Dad's permission. The truck driver who drove me here was an Anglican from Stratford with a family. He wouldn't have harmed me, and I won't be running around London, to quote Dad. The nuns have very strict rules about curfew. They treat us like family. The other girls are very hard working and friendly. You would like them. I'm very happy here. Maybe I sinned by going against my parents' wishes, but at what age is a person supposed to become an adult, make decisions? I am determined to make something of myself, Jack.

You'll never guess! I am training for birthing and tending babies! I can't believe my luck in landing a post in the maternity ward, my first choice. New life is the best antidote to fearing the future. One night I showed up for my shift and was rushed into a room where a woman who couldn't speak English had just arrived and was ready to pop the cork, as they say. I happened to stand at the foot of the bed where I could see the whole miracle unfold. That baby arrived very fast; she just slipped into the world, gave a gurgle and a cry. So that's what all the fuss is about, I thought. That little child was perfect, and so tiny. We counted ten fingers and toes for the mother who understood our message and couldn't stop smiling.

I decided then and there that maternity is the ward for me. I spoke to Sister Margaret and she agreed to post me here for the time being. If I behave, I can stay. So I'm working on my behaviour! Sister's exact words were, "Mary, dear, calm down! We have to remain open to serve wherever God calls us; however, I believe you could develop into an excellent maternity nurse. You have a lot of heart, Mary, so bless our babies with your passion, but also your training." I left her office on a cloud.

I forgot to mention that when we graduated each of us was awarded a gold pin. Mine has "Mary Calder, 1940" engraved on the back. I'm going to keep it forever.

You must have arrived overseas by now. I want to hear all about crossing the Atlantic Ocean (Wow!) and what England looks like. You have to write very descriptive letters, Jack, so we can imagine your life over there. Big hugs and bags of love,
Mary xoxo

Dear Jack,   **Apr. 1, 1941**

I have some news from this side of the ocean. Your mother and I are moving to the parish of St. George's in Owen Sound. The Bishop thinks I have a way with finances and that particular congregation needs to be built up. The present minister is not necessarily talented at raising money and the Bishop thinks, in his words, "More could be done." I don't really know what I can do to help; people are feeling the pinch of war as their household budgets shrink They try to buy War Bonds with their little bit of savings, or send money overseas to airmen, soldiers and sailors, so what's left to support the Bishop's dreams is anyone's guess.

Apparently the Bishop heard word (he won't say from whom) that I am 'a gifted orator.' Well, I'm blushing, but I guess my love of making speeches in the Legislature has a ripple effect. Maybe I will be able to lift the spirits of the people here.

Your mother is not too happy about another move. She tends to set down roots in a community more than I do, and after only six years in Goderich, it's hard for her to tear herself away. She is such a great supporter of my work and people always fall in love with her as soon as they meet her. She's naturally warm and funny in a way that I cannot muster. People like me for my fine sermons, but they love your mother. The sixteen years we had in Chatham when you children were small were the best for her.

The Bishop has ordered us to move in four weeks and I think that would be best for all concerned. Best for your mother not to linger and weep over losing friendships. Best to move on and establish new friendships to heal the broken heart.

People here supported us through the loss of our Gerald. Their kindness and understanding will never be forgotten. Gerald is buried here so we will always come back to visit his grave. I don't believe his spirit resides here, but memories are freshest here and worth nurturing as they are all that we have left of our boy. I realize I have begun to forget the little things about his childhood. I can still hear his voice, however, and that is a comfort. He used to call me Da, as if the Gaelic ancestral voices were strong in him. It's late at night that I miss him most and I often turn to his journals and his poetry. Some of his phrases are quite stunning.

If you could write something special to your mother, that would be helpful at this time. Must go and help her pack another box. Love, *Dad*

PS There was a rather nice piece written in *The Border Cities Star*, Windsor, regarding the announcement of my transfer. I think it has the same bones as the piece they published about me in 1935 when I arrived! I'm enclosing it for your amusement.

RECTOR GOES TO OWEN SOUND
REV. A.C. CALDER WILL LEAVE
ST. GEORGE'S, GODERICH
AFTER 6 YEARS
FORMER M.L.A. NOTED FOR
ORATORY AND GOOD WORKS
IN COUNTY

Goderich, April 1— Offered the parish of St. George's Owen Sound, the Rev. A.C. Calder, L.L.B., B.A., former member of the Ontario Provincial legislature for West Kent, and Rector of St. George's, Goderich announced yesterday that he has accepted the new charge.

SURPRISE TO FRIENDS

The move will terminate 6 years of active service both within St. George's parish and in the wider community.

The announcement, which came as a surprise to his congregation and to the many friends in Goderich, was made by Mr. Calder from the pulpit during both morning and evening services. Mr. Calder will leave to assume his new duties on May 1.

Goderich loses a man who has given many years of his life to community and provincial service.

TWICE VICTORIOUS

A Conservative in politics, Mr. Calder carried the blue banner to victory in the provincial elections in 1926 and again in 1929. During his terms as West Kent's representative, he became known for his ability as an orator and for his fine knowledge of the English language. In Chatham and Kent County, and also throughout the province while in the legislature, he often spoke in other ridings on behalf of Conservative candidates, and on many occasions, assumed the role of after-dinner speaker.

KNOWS ROOSEVELT

He was born on Campobello Island, NB, the son of James and Martha Calder, United Empire Loyalist stock. It was during his boyhood that Mr. Calder became intimately acquainted with Franklin Delano Roosevelt, President of the United States, when the president as a boy spent summers with his family at the Roosevelt family home.

Mr. Calder attended Superior School on Campobello, and later entered the NB Normal School, from which he obtained a First Class Teacher's Certificate.

For a short period he taught school, and then entered Dalhousie University, Halifax, NS, from which he graduated in Law in 1902. After practising in his profession for a period of 4 years, he gave up that profession to enter the University of Bishop's

College at Lennoxville, PQ. His decision to enter the ministry took him to remote corners of Canada where he established missionary headquarters.

Following his ordination he went to Last Mountain Country in Saskatchewan, where he established a missionary post. After 3 years he was made Rector of the pre-Cathedral in Qu'Appelle. After transferring to the diocese of Huron, he served as Rector of St. James', Wallaceburg (3 years), and Holy Trinity, Chatham (15 years) where he also found time to be Chairman of the Board of Education.

Dear Dad,   May 1, 1941

Congratulations on your move to Owen Sound. I've never been there so you'll have to tell me all about it. The Bishop's confidence in you is flattering. Don't let it go to your head!

I have been doing some thinking with respect to our last discussion. Here are some points that I think you will find interesting:

It has been a revelation to me that England is not falling apart at the seams and is still green and beautiful in the spring. London has been battered badly, all right, but buildings in London don't make up Briton any more than buildings make up a church or a university. What's more, one gets a pretty good idea by travelling around of the stuff of which England is made. We saw it in the eyes of children in a north country city when we tossed them Canadian pennies and they shouted, "Hello Canada! It's good to see you!" We saw it when we went into the underground stations in London and old women sat up in their rude beds to exclaim: "Hello Canada! Ain't we the lucky ones!"

When we went to tea with the Royal Family, the Queen was telling of her visit to the bombed-out areas of London East that morning. "Those women just shook their fists and said, 'If only we could get that man.'" The Queen told me, "They're so brave."

I came to England a little doubtful about some of the stories I had heard of Britons' courage under this ordeal. Surely, I thought, there'll be grumbling that isn't just the old wartime grumbling, and there'll be signs of weakening. Yet the people here can never be praised sufficiently and the true story of their spirit can never be put into words. As Churchill says, "It is refreshing just to go among them."

These people won't be beaten. They never will. All I hope is that the signs of increasing aid from the United States continue to pile up. No one here is hungry, but there will be hungry mouths unless the Battle of the Atlantic is won this year. Canadians can't begin to realise how necessary it is that the two sides of the Atlantic be brought closer and closer together and that the flow of goods grows greater and greater — with no questions asked about when payment is to be made. Anyone who knows anything at all about the potentialities of aircraft knows that this is as much North America's war as England's, if you want to look at it from a purely materialistic standpoint.

Oh, there are people here who just try to get away from it all, just the same as people decide to stop paying insurance premiums because they need the money for bingo. But I haven't talked with anyone yet who isn't prepared to kick the living hell out of any German who sets foot on British soil. So, Father, what I'm trying to say is, could you pass along word to your congregation and your political friends, to support the war effort and to write to their American cousins to help us out, the sooner the better.

We had a very quiet, pleasant trip over. Sonny Morse and Don McIntyre from Chatham were aboard and we spent a good deal of time together.

The visit to Windsor Castle grounds was the thrill of a lifetime. We had been told not to expect to meet any of the Royal Family. When the King and Queen and the Princesses walked into the reception room, preceded by their two prancing, barking dogs, you could have knocked out the fifty-five of us with the Royal Sceptre. As senior officer, I had to introduce the Canadians and as a result I chatted for quite a while with all the members of the family. The King was keenly interested in our training. The Queen recalled her 1939 visit to Canada. The Princesses were willing to joke about anything and everything. As one of the air gunners put it afterward: "Just let me get a German in my sights now." I never met a more charming family or a family that was more genuinely eager to be kind to visitors in the home.

And now I'm set down on a station outside a pretty little English village. After two nights in London with the Canadian Press boys, both my pocketbook and I are ready to plunge deep into hard work.

Love to all, *Jack*

PS I hear Mary entered nursing at St. Joe's in London. Good for her. She's just the gal for that career. And Marjorie, I hear from former colleagues, is well liked in the Toronto CP office. She'll do well there. Please don't forget to take Char for her walks and scratch her on the head for me. I miss her.

PILOT OFFICER CALDER PRESENTS HIS COMRADES TO THE KING AND QUEEN

Former Chatham boy, and once a member of the editorial staff of the Chatham Daily News, is cautious when Queen asks how many airmen arrived in England in contingent of flyers trained under Empire scheme.

Several Chatham men were in

Dear Mom, May 15, 1941

I hope you are adjusting to your new home. I don't know much about the town so you'll have to describe it to me. Thank you for your recent letter with news of everyone back in Goderich. It is so good to hear of all the opportunities you have in Owen Sound too. The socks will arrive in due course and will be the envy of the whole squadron, I'm sure! I'll tell all the boys that you knit with your eyes shut, or while conducting a meeting of the Ladies' Auxiliary. None of us could thread a needle when we arrived in England but now we have to mend our own, so needs must.

How is Dad? How does the new congregation respond to him? I suppose he's as busy as ever writing sermons and speeches. Tell him I miss our debates. Most of all I miss my talks with you late at night in the screened porch. Remember the thunderstorms we used to watch as they rolled in off Lake Huron? I dream of the day we'll be together again watching those wonderful sunsets at the cottage, all eight of us sitting around the campfire at Inverhuron, Jake on his banjo and Phil trying to keep up on the harmonica, Mary and Marjorie and you singing so beautifully, everyone chiming in with stories and jokes. How corny we were! I think our family must carry the gene for puns and terrible witty remarks. The lads here frequently slap me up the side of my head when we have some leave time. They tease me about my red hair and freckles, so I have to fire back something at them. All in good fun.

As for my life here, the excitement of new learning never stops. Honestly Mom, we are being so well prepared in terms of fitness, our minds sharp and alert all day, and we are developing a great sense of camaraderie such as I have rarely experienced.

Do you remember Bobby Keefer, the football player from McGill I met in Montreal? I wrote about him when I was covering sports for CP. You'll never guess: we ran into each other on the Atlantic crossing and vowed to stay close. He is becoming a real friend; we think alike in so many ways, and he has a great sense of humour. Our three months in the British Commonwealth Air Training Plan seemed very long, as we're all anxious to get going and give those Nazis a knock-out punch they'll never forget.

You will be surprised to see my picture in the papers soon announcing my promotion to the rank of Pilot Officer. Very grand, eh. And another story will shock you: your son met the King and Queen and Princesses Elizabeth and Margaret Rose. Actually, we had just finished our training and were treated to a tour of Windsor Castle Gardens, when who should appear but the Royal family. They had motored back from wherever they were to meet the Canadians. And they invited us for tea.

Say, do you listen to Vera Lynn? Her songs are piped into the barracks once a week from her radio show and we all derive great comfort from her lyrics. Her voice could melt butter. It doesn't hurt that she must be one of the prettiest girls in England. All the boys plan to see her when she performs in London.

Well, it's nearly time for lights out. To answer your question, our cots are quite comfortable and we have clean sheets once a week. Love to all, *Jack*

Dear Mom, May 28, 1941

You would have loved flying with me today. We are nearing the end of our training, so we had a more or less free day to fly over Northern England and even over Scotland and Wales, in a big circle. Each country is different from the others. England has miles and miles of small green fields surrounded by hedgerows, villages each with its church spire. Wales is remarkable for its mountains where the coal miners eke out a living. The towns have a dark tone, I suppose from the coal dust. The poverty is evident from the air. Scotland, on the other hand, is brilliant and colourful. Its mountains are covered with golden gorse. I'm planning a hiking holiday there the next time I'm on leave.

Bob and I are sharing a room and training together. We have a small coal stove in the middle of the room which keeps the hut fairly comfortable. We often share mugs of tea late at night sitting around the stove before bed. In fact, that's where I am now, so you can picture me. I'm in the peak of health as I'm sure we are served the best bacon and eggs in the country. The meals in the mess are hearty and we are given lunch packs to take on each trip if we are going to be away for hours. Our laundry is done for us, even ironing and boot polishing; whereas the NCOs must do their own, poor sods! It's worth being an officer in this war, I'm telling you. My university education is paying off in a new way.

Some of the boys over here have serious girlfriends back home, and some are getting into serious relationships over here. Mom, I have decided not to say anything that could be interpreted as a promise to a girl until the war is over. When we go on leave I just want to be light hearted and have fun. I don't want any girl pining for me while I'm on ops; that wouldn't be fair. I know other fellows think differently. They want to live it up and experience love because they might not live to see tomorrow, but I am optimistic that my future will be bright once we give Jerry a good knock-out punch. This is a job we have to get done first.

Our training officers all have experience on ops so they know what they're talking about. I'm learning every day. Bob is a good pilot. He and I are thick as a team, together with the other five in our crew. They are awesome lads. We look out for each other.

Sorry that this letter is wandering all over the place but it's been a long day, even though an exhilarating one of a long practice flight. I navigated well enough to touch all points on the map we had marked and get us back to the aerodrome in time for supper.

I hear that Mary has enrolled in the nursing programme in London. Honestly, Mom, I know you are disappointed that she is not at home with you to help out, but I think she made a smart move. She's old enough to think for herself and she just wants the same chance at life that we all have. I think she'll make a right proper nurse. If I ever crash, I'd want someone like her by my bedside.

Bob sends best wishes to you and Dad. He promises to bring me home safely. Love to all, *Jack*

Dear Dad, June 8, 1941

A few weeks ago I was on leave in Scotland. I had a lovely time hiking near Fort William with my pilot, Bobby Keefer. We were singing "It's a long way to Tipperary" as we marched over hill and dale. We drove here in his Uncle Wilks' '35 Hudson convertible which Bobby bought for £10. We coaxed some petrol tickets from our boss in exchange for a large bottle of Uncle Wilks' Canadian Club rye (Keefer, *Grounded*, 212).

Dad, I know you didn't grow up in Scotland but your father did. Do you know what town your grandfather came from? Why did he leave Scotland? I never thought to ask you.

We were invited into a local home and were surprised to see a large cage in the middle of the LR floor. This house is home to 2 extra children who have been evacuated from London and are living with their aunt and uncle for the duration of the war. Very charming children, 9 and 12, a girl and a boy. Very inquisitive, wanted to know all about Canada, and flying. They told me that they sleep in the cage every night with auntie and uncle in case of a bomb. I thought, quietly to myself, that a cage wouldn't help much, but they explained that if a bomb fell nearby and shook the house so badly that it caved in and they were inside the cage, the wardens and neighbours would come and dig them out and if they were under the cage it would catch the falling debris and save their lives and when the war is over they will see their mommy and daddy again. My heart breaks that children have to have such thoughts in their heads.

I learned later that the cage is called a Morrison shelter, the roof of which can be used as a table. How very practical. There's another kind of shelter which has become popular. It consists of sheets of corrugated steel welded together, something like a mini-Quonset hut in shape. People assemble them and sink them into the ground in their garden, what we would call their back yard. They pour a cement floor with a hole in the middle for the water to drain because of course it rains a LOT in England. That one is an Anderson shelter. Both these shelters are meant to house 6 people in the event of an air raid and are provided by the government to people earning less than £350/yr.

Of course you've probably heard of many Londoners running into the Tube stations whenever the air raid sirens scream. In the beginning of the war, this crowding was forbidden for fear of disease, but the people pushed their way in anyway and eventually the government supported the idea, even supplying bunk beds and chemical toilets. I heard one story about an airman who wandered into a Tube station during a raid and people stood up and cheered for him, exhorting him to knock out Hitler's teeth!

I hear a lot of stories like that, Dad. Who knows whether they are true or not, but they circulate the way jokes do. Sometimes when we're enjoying a pint or two in a pub someone will tell one of these stories, then someone else tries to top it by telling an even more unbelievable story, and so it goes for the rest of the night until all the pints run dry and it's time for bed.

Then we all climb on our bicycles and weave our way home through the blackout. If there's no moon the dark is unbelievably black, such dark as I've never seen. Sometimes we try to use flashlights, but only until the warden catches us. Well, flashlights aren't actually much help when you're wobbling along on a rickety old bike that you bought from some bloke for 2 bob. A few chaps, like Bobby, are lucky enough to find an old car. The worst part of owning a vehicle is the begging one is subjected to from all one's friends and acquaintances who wish to hitch a ride, some of whom don't even offer to pay for gas. Because of this, a kind of bartering often happens by the side of the road after a pub night: chaps bidding for rides. If they land a ride, they'll sell the bike they arrived on to some lowly chap. So the bikes circulate. Sometimes a guy will ride home a better bike than he arrived on. It's that way with raincoats and umbrellas in Canada, don't you think?

So, Dad, how are things going for you? I imagine it must be hard to deliver a positive sermon when there's a war on. How do you handle the killing? I'd be interested to learn how you preach the gospel these days. And please feel free to fill me in on the political scene at home, and of course the scores. I miss reading the papers. My bailiwick of course was sports writing for CP. How is Mary doing in nursing? Dad, I know you didn't approve when she left home, but she's grown up now and has to make her way in the world. She'll be married all too soon. She's such a pretty girl and won't stay single for long once the boys come home from war, so I say: let her experience a career for a little while. When she passes her exams, she'll make a wonderful nurse. That's my opinion, which you didn't ask for.

I hear from Jake regularly. He's enjoying instructing, but then he always did have the gift of the gab. Am I telling tales if I say that I think he's found a girl? I'll leave you with that thought to ponder. Love to all, *Jack*

Dear Mom, June 9, 1941

I was glad to receive three of your letters in the post recently. I don't know how the postal service is managing with the volume of mail since the war began, but from this end it seems very erratic. Some letters and packages get to the intended recipient and some go astray. Sadly, I hear that some are lost forever to the bottom of the Atlantic. But I also hear that the powers above my pay grade are working on solutions so that people on both sides of the sea will be able to stay in touch. That is so important for everyone's morale, isn't it? I have even heard a rumour that a special air convoy is being dedicated to the mail. Imagine that, a whole plane load chock full of letters. Something like Santa Claus forms in my imagination. I know that most of the boys here are writing letters regularly because I see them huddled over pen and paper outside the mess hall. Sometimes we are ordered to fly a mission; we get dressed and show up, only to be told to wait because the weather has closed in. Everyone grabs a bit of privacy to write home. And of course, our commanding officers recommend that we keep in touch with loved ones.

This letter will find its way to you in Owen Sound. You will have been there for a month now. How are you settling in? What is the congregation like? Tell me about the rectory. I hope it is as wonderful as our home in Chatham. I will always have fond memories of sneaking out Jake's bedroom window, crawling over the sunroom roof and down the rose trellis when we were teens.

I received your care package. You must have mailed it before you left Goderich. Thank you, dear Mother, from the bottom of my heart. You're an angel. My reputation around this place went up considerably when the boys tasted your marmalade. We all share each other's packages so I had to bring out the marmalade when it was time for toast last night. We don't see oranges here now what with rationing. I'm keeping the socks for myself! My favourite colour too, like the sky and the sea. You are the best mother ever.

We hear some interesting accents around the aerodrome. 1) A Scottish instructor who has such a burr in his tongue that we can't understand the names he's pronouncing, and we're supposed to be able to navigate to these places. We do make fun of him behind his back. Anything for a little levity. 2) The Polish boys who escaped from Russia. They still have manacle marks around their wrists, and tell of being shipped in open cattle cars in winter dressed only in summer clothing. 3) The Turks who are wizard at flying Spitfires, and luckily they crew up with each other because nobody else can understand them. 4) Believe it or not there are quite a few Irish from both north and south who have come across the Irish Sea to join up. Even though Ireland is neutral, many folks there believe that we have to knock out Jerry or he'll walk on water to take over their ports too. Of course you must know about the bombing of Dublin in January. I thought for sure that would convince southern Ireland to join the Allies, but no. Their PM, de Valera, is stubbornly set against Britain and won't lift a finger to help.

I'm learning my trade as a navigator. They divided us officers into groups depending on our skills and mine seem to fall towards mathematics, both lineal and spatial. However there's a huge difference between navigating the ground in Canada where most of the roads go north/south or east/west and here where they run higgledy-piggledy all over the place, around in circles, over hill and dale. I don't think they ever heard of blasting a rock out of the way to create space for a road, no. They drive around the rock as if they are still riding in carriages. From the air one can really see how crazy the roads look. No wonder it takes so long to go anywhere at all. Riding home on a bicycle in a black out is especially challenging! I can hear you chuckling as you're reading this.

Mom, I don't want you worrying about anything. I am well cared for, well trained, well supported by my crew. Couldn't ask for a better bunch of lads. And Bobby is a superb pilot and leader. I think they throw all the rations at us boys 'on the front lines,' as they say, so we are well fed. Last week a local widow, Mrs. Wilson, invited a bunch of us into her lovely home for a home-cooked meal. She served meatloaf, mashed potatoes with gravy, and peas, with peach crumble for dessert. I could have closed my eyes and imagined being with you at home.

I hope you and Dad will be able to find new partners for bridge games in Goderich. You must still have some fun even though there's a war. Don't let your spirits lag. And remember to send me the odd joke. The boys do enjoy a laugh when I have a new one to share.

I was on leave in Scotland recently so be sure to read the letter I wrote to Dad about that. Over and out for now, dear one. Love to all, *Jack*

Dear Mom, June 15, 1941

I've had letters from Mary and Marjorie and both seem happy in their new occupations. Phil came to see me for my birthday (thanks for the $50!). I guess he's been busy. When he was here I was able to exchange duties with another navigator (for an easy run across the channel). Bob didn't mind. Phil and I grabbed a train to London for a show at the Opera House. We saw Noel Coward's *Blithe Spirit*. Outstanding. I don't know if you have heard of it but if you have a chance, do see it. We both enjoyed the money you sent, so thanks again. I took him out to Minsky's after the theatre and introduced him to all the boys. Phil was in top form with his dry wit. He can certainly hold his own when there's a bunch of us throwing remarks around the table. I must say he looked very smart in his new uniform. Hard to get my head around the fact that my little brother is a soldier. He was keen to see some action so he's probably knocking on Hitler's door at this very moment. I'm sure he can take care of himself. He is a bright boy and very quick on his feet. He can almost outrun me, but not quite! My legs are longer.

Rationing is rather tight over here. The locals have invented a meatless pie which is actually quite tasty. Since FDR signed the Lend Lease Act into US law allowing the Americans to supply Britain with military equipment, it is looking increasingly as if the US will join the Allies, so LOOK OUT Nazis! Plus our boys on the sea captured a German sub INTACT, i.e. with all its toys undamaged. Morale is very high these days and we feel the tide is turning in our favour.

There's some political news I'm hearing chatter about. I wonder, if you see any press release about the William Beveridge Report, could you let me know? Keep an eye on the headlines over there because I'd like to know the reaction to Churchill's statements. You're sure to have a more balanced report on the Report (!) than we will get here.

We are seeing some interesting war posters. There's a campaign on to engage the whole country in keeping gossip about troop movements quiet. Sayings like "Loose lips sink ships" and "Careless talk costs lives" appear on posters with cartoon images of women. Of course the fact that women are subtly being accused is causing controversy just when the war effort needs women to support industries. I saw an amusing one in the train station: A cartoon of Hitler's ear is drawn to look super large and the slogan goes: "Hitler wants to know the unit's name, where it's going, whence it came. Ships, guns, and shells all make him curious. Silence makes him Feuhrious!" I hate to think of spies lurking in our midst but I suppose it's always wise to be careful. There's another poster that hits the nail on the head. Popeye is ready to punch the lights out of a big guy for talking too much. Warning across the bottom says: "It's taboo to mention sailing dates." Sad but true that some of our boys have lost their lives in the navy.

You know, Mom, I have the greatest respect for sailors, but I really feel safer in the skies. Our jacket patch with the RCAF slogan says: "Per adua ad astra" (through adversity to the stars). We have control over our aircraft and our crew is very sharp. I love flying and I believe in our mission. God must be on our side! We have to fight this war on all fronts. Your support is very much appreciated. Socks, marmalade, tins of salmon, letters — all make a difference. I feel that I am very lucky, lucky in my family and in the wonderful friendships I have formed. Love to all, *Jack*

Dear Jack,   **June 26, 1941**

How are you? Your mother and I read your letters with great interest, especially when they first arrive from the mailman, and then in the evening, we often read them over again. They are a great comfort. Even just to touch the same paper as you have held in your hand is a blessing for your mother. Indeed, she said so last night. I must confess that I feel the same. Now that she has said it aloud, I feel the truth of it for myself too. So strange, ironic, that this violent war has had the power to crack me open and reveal to myself a tenderness for you boys that I don't really know how to express. It's hard for me to admit, and you might not hear your father say this ever again, but there it is, in plain language, black and white, staring at me. Your mother and I have led busy lives, outside of parenting six children. To be honest, I think you lot brought yourselves up; maybe your mother and I guided you a little from time to time, but basically you became typical preacher's kids, running wild. Now I find myself wishing I had spent more time with you — throwing a ball around, or singing. What would it have hurt? We did have wonderful debates though, didn't we. You have developed into an intelligent thinker, an articulate writer, and for those skills I am particularly proud.

I am freshly home from the spring Synod. The Bishop gave a very sobering and, at the same time, uplifting "Charge," mainly about the war facing us. Canadians express gratitude that "it could not happen here." However, the battle is really ours. The prize in this struggle is control of the Americas. Whoever holds control here will ultimately control the world.

More people are attending church services. If they don't have sons or even daughters away at the front, everyone knows someone whose offspring or father, cousin or uncle, is absent from home. I see the tears in their eyes as I look out from the pulpit, and often I have to exert control over my voice lest I betray my personal feelings. I have a responsibility to lead them and I take that very solemnly. I don't think I've ever spoken to you before of my passion for the ministry. It's strange how close you are to me tonight even though we're separated by an ocean.

There is an awakening perception of what the Church stands for. Ordinarily we take our liberty, the value of the individual, and a thousand other things that form our common heritage, as matters of course. When they are threatened, we become aware that they are God's gifts to us.

Of course, the Bishop sees the Church and the Christian Gospel at the heart of all of history and interprets worldly events in that light, as do I, most of the time. I do not have his clarity of vision, however, and for that I rely upon these annual visits to Synod. I wish I could see God's hand in this war. I find it hard when my three remaining sons are caught up in a battle I cannot see. I only hear news reports from afar, crackling over the radio. You, and Jake, and Philip are my touchstones for the reality of this horrible thing that has us all in its grip. How can one evil, power-hungry mere man have gained so much control so fast? He shits the same as I do, and yet I dare say his soul is of a different mold.

The Bishop praised the amazing British people for their marvellous spirit. He said, "They stand as the bulwark of civilization, the front line of the battle for North America." I think Winston Churchill quoted him, or was it the other way around? No matter; it's true.

I'm tired after an intense session at the conference. I need to "think on these things," as the letter to the Philippians advises. I simply wanted to write to you before going to bed.

The Bishop is organizing a tangible gift from the Church to all the sons and daughters of Anglicans who are serving in uniform. It will be a simple cross which can be pinned beneath your tunic as a reminder at all times that our Lord has not forgotten you. These will be arriving in a month or two, mailed to the chaplains who will distribute them to the appropriate candidates. In fact, I think I will ask him to send a few thousand crosses so that every soldier, sailor, and airman who wants one shall have one. Why not ask the other churches to join us in supporting this endeavour.

I know your mother sends her love, as always.

Imagine that I'm cheering for the home team just the same as when I was standing on the sidelines and you flew by with the ball in your hands. Love, *Dad*

Dear Jack, June 30, 1941

Hope this letter finds you well, my dear son. I think of you all the time and pray that you will be safe in the air and on the ground, with bombs everywhere around you. Please be careful. You don't have to take undo risks to do your job over there.

Your father is worn down with widows and mothers, sisters and friends leaning on him, asking for words of wisdom and he really honestly feels some days he has nothing to offer. Oh he offers the psalms usually, and the sayings of Jesus, but in his heart he is at a loss to understand how God fits in. He trudges around town from one sad door to another after he has read the lists of "missing and lost" on the bulletin board at the post office. He knows their sorrow keenly since we lost Gerald only three years ago. You understand it too, I know, more so because Gerald was visiting you when he was killed in that freak car accident. I only mention it because your father won't talk about Gerald at all any more. It's as if he disappeared. Your father's approach to death is that it is a mystery known only to God and we do not question His wisdom. But I question it, God forgive me. Why do the young die before they have even lived? How do you deal with death, Jack, you and your pals who see those empty chairs in the mess whenever you come home from ops?

I almost tore this letter to shreds when I read it over, but we must face these issues, I feel. Now, on a more cheerful note, I have a couple of jokes for you lads.

Four paratroopers each from England, Scotland, France and the US, were on a plane about to jump when they realized there was only one serviceable parachute.

The French paratrooper downed a glass of cognac, said "Pour la France!" and jumped without the parachute.

The American downed a glass of bourbon, said "For freedom!" and jumped without the parachute.

The Scotsman downed a glass of whiskey, said "For Scotland!" and threw out the Englishman.

A British Commando unit was waiting to go behind enemy lines into Norway.

During the planning of the mission, it was decided that their rifles would need protective covers against the extreme cold of Norway. The contract to manufacture the covers was given to a pharmaceutical company that also manufactured condoms.

Before the Commandos deployed, Winston Churchill personally inspected them. He was shown a box of the newly-made protective covers. "Won't do," he said gruffly.

The Prime Minister searched through all of the other boxes. "No, won't do at all."

"But sir!" protested the mission commander. "They're exactly the right size for the rifles! Ten-and-a-half inches!"

"Labels," said Churchill. "I want every one of these boxes labelled 'British, Size: Medium.' If anyone's captured, we'll show the Jerries who's the bloody Master Race."

Don't tell your father I gave you that joke. We were playing bridge last Friday when Bill Bowers told us that one. We all laughed but your father wouldn't approve of my passing it along.

Well, it's time to head to the kitchen. We're lucky tonight. A man from the market who knows your father brought us a piece of mutton, so I'm stretching the leftovers to make shepherd's pie.

We love you, dear boy, and are so proud of you for doing your bit. Never mind my dark thoughts. Love, *Mom xo*

Dear Mom and Dad, July 10, 1941

I think of you back home in that big house. You both are very involved in community work, so I want to try to describe for you my life as a flyer.

Sometimes we are skimming across the waves of the English Channel; sometimes we fly high and then swoop down to the target, and then full throttle up again banking away from the flak. Flying is the most amazing experience and I hope you both have a chance go up into the air when the war is over.

Mom, you asked how we deal with the empty chairs in the mess. Honestly, we raise a glass and then get back to work. If anything, we are more motivated to get the ones who ultimately caused their deaths, the Nazis, the Luftwaffe, Goering and Hitler. We fly ops every chance we get and when we've rested, we party. That's the truth of it. We're frightfully busy. The only time for reflection is between the briefing and take-off, that unhappy hour when there's nothing to do but wait for the green light from the control tower. Some of the lads play cards, but I prefer to write in my journal. We can't think too long about the empty chairs because if we did, we might not have the guts to go back out there day after day. We understand that there's a lot of skill involved in flying, but there's also luck. Mom, Dad, you know me; you know I've always done my best at whatever I tried and I usually come out smelling like a rose. This is challenging work but I love flying, we have a crackerjack crew, and I'm a good navigator! So, pray for me with a smile.

Dad, our wing commander often has to visit the widows to tell them the news. It's not a job I envy and I hear from Mom that you are taking on that responsibility back home. Even if you can't always find the words, just being there to listen and offer support is a very big thing. Your experience in the valley goes before you when you visit. People know you're not there to offer platitudes. When you say you understand, they know from whence you come. 'Gerald' says it all.

I think of Gerald every day. I feel very close to him when I am amongst the stars, being flung through the skies at 200 miles an hour. Dad, I know Heaven is a mystery, it's not a physical place, but we do have hours on ops when we're not doing much. We're on course and we just have to watch for landmarks and basically wait until we arrive. I find my thoughts turning to Gerald and all the fun we had together growing up, the crazy times we embarrassed you with our boyhood pranks. I blame

Jake, as he was the eldest, and Philip just tried to keep up. Gerald was the quiet one who came along out of loyalty. He was my gentle brother who loved to read and keep a journal and write poetry. I wish I had listened to him more instead of yammering at him with my own ideas. You see, he's with me as I fly.

I miss you both. Write soon. Love to all, *Jack*

Dear Dad,   **1 August, 1941**

I received your letter dated June 26. Thank you for your outpouring of honesty and love. Just because you were not demonstrative with hugs and valentines doesn't mean we didn't feel your love. Of course we respected you, even feared you on occasion when we thought we might get caught for something wild or naughty, but we always detected that twinkle in your eye and half smile at the side of your mouth that betrayed your true feelings. Your secret is safe with us, Dad.

Thanks for news from home. I enjoy hearing your ideas, even if you are practising your sermons! That's fair, because I'm practising my journalism. We never shied away from debate at home, did we?

Do you want to know why I think we're fighting this war? You've told me your opinion; now here's a slice of mine. We have our propaganda here too and this much I agree with: we're fighting against naked aggression which is led by a dictator of unusual popularity. Apparently, he is an inspiring speaker, capable of rousing crowds to a frenzy. Those who hear him become hysterical, whipped up by malignant sayings he shouts, which they in turn chant, pumping their fists in the air. He quotes so called wrongs committed against the German people and they believe him. He fires people up to such emotion that they have lost the ability to think for themselves, and follow him blindly. On marches across country, German soldiers commit unspeakable crimes: murder, rape, and pillage. It's true: the

Nazis have lost their humanity. They've lost their compassion. They're blind animals.

Dad, I get very worked up when I think about what might happen if we don't stop Hitler's advance. And if he conquers Britain, what's to stop him from coming for North America? Think of it: you and Mom are in grave danger if we don't stop the Jerries here. There's a line drawn across the English Channel beyond which they'd better not go. We will stop them, Dad. You can count on us. No matter what you hear over there, Dad, we in the RAF know that the Luftwaffe ME-109s, while formidable, actually run out of fuel and turn back before they finish the air fight they came to accomplish!

We hear horrible stories from those who have escaped and risked their lives to cross the channel and join us, stories of innocent people imprisoned; some even shot or hanged, no trial, no judge. Early on, the RAF received injections of hundreds of Polish aircrew. They are brilliant fliers, daring fighters, because they have seen the enemy up close. The lowest impulses known throughout history are being unleashed in Europe by the Jerries. Believe me, Dad, because I've heard it from eyewitnesses.

The Nazis have taken control of newspapers and radio stations to perpetrate their lies and propaganda. The German people are so besotted with their leader that they do not respond with indignation to these atrocities. They have lost their courage; they won't stand up to him. Dad, my blood boils sometimes and I am sorry to say I am so filled with outrage that it verges on hate. Is it hate, Dad, hate that is unforgivable in God's eyes? When we fight against a monster, is not God outraged too? Or maybe He is just sad that this beautiful world He imagined has dissolved into a field of slaughter.

Fascism has spread its terror across Europe with blinding speed and Hitler has his eye on Britain. We must use every tool to win, including bombs. I confess to you that we don't always hit our targets. In truth, when we bombed Berlin, sadly, we hit the suburbs. We fly most missions at night as that is safest for us, and when there are fewer civilians working in the factories. The Jerries were hitting our aerodromes pretty severely, but now Goering has turned his attention to bombing London, Coventry, Dublin — he's deliberately murdering civilians. We see news reels of the damage done in the bombed out cities. It's not just propaganda; it's real, recent film, some of it made by guys I used to work with at CP. I know for a fact that it's not doctored.

In Churchill's opinion the only thing that could bring down Hitler is "an absolutely devastating exterminating attack by very heavy bombers from this country upon the Nazi homeland."

Dad, when this war is over, and we return to Canada, I want you to meet some of the boys I've been working with, to hear their point of view, listen to their stories. I cannot tell you how highly I prize their work ethic and their friendship. I've never known such strong ties with men. If you were here and could see the picture first-hand, you would be proud of the work we're doing.

Frankly I don't know how you can preach the Gospel in these times. It must be hard to balance reality with the Word. I'm always interested to know your thoughts, Dad, so keep the letters flowing. Love to all, *Jack*

PS I'm including a clipping from *The Daily Express* in which our Commander in Chief Arthur Harris is quoted. Our recent bombing strategy might be hard for you to hear.

> Harris: "If I could send a thousand bombers to Germany every night, it would end the war by autumn. We are going to bomb Germany incessantly ... the day is coming when the USA and ourselves will put over such a force that the Germans will scream for mercy."
>
> Personal message to crews from Harris: "The force of which you form a part tonight is a least twice the size and has more than four times the carrying capacity of the largest air force ever before concentrated on one objective. You have an

opportunity, therefore, to strike a blow at the enemy which will resound not only throughout Germany, but throughout the world. In your hands lie the means of destroying a major part of the resources by which the enemy's war effort is maintained. It depends, however, on each individual crew whether full concentration is achieved. Press home your attack to your precise objective with the utmost determination and resolution in the foreknowledge that, if you individually succeed, the most shattering and devastating blow will have been delivered against the very vitals of the enemy. Let him have it — right on the chin."

Dear Mom,   Aug. 13, 1941

I think of you every day. Even when I'm engaged on a mission there are moments that my mind drifts toward family. You are like a magnet for me, my true north. How are Marjorie and Mary? I hear from Marjorie now and again, but Mary, not so much. I suppose nursing calls for long hours. We will sit down to dinner together some Sunday in the future, I'm counting on that.

    Philip dropped in for a visit before he left for duties. We had a serious talk about his future after the war. I think he might be headed for journalism too. That will make three of us. Maybe Jake will find a career with us as he certainly has the gift of the gab and wouldn't be shy about interviewing anybody, rich, famous, or down-and-out. I can picture him with a microphone striding up to the Prime Minister at a train station, pencil and pad in hand. With Philip's interest in history, I think he could find a place as a foreign correspondent, living in Europe after the war.

    Once we've put Hitler to bed, and I do mean permanently, Europe will regenerate. This is why we're bombing it now, to put a stop to this madness. I don't understand why anybody believes his lies about a master race. What utter bunk. Hitler is astonishing; the way he took over Europe takes the breath away.

His goal is world domination. He must be stopped. I have no qualms about bombing in order to stop him.

In a few days you will see an article of mine in the papers describing a bombing raid I participated in. To be more accurate, our crew was chosen to lead the op, which was a pretty safe position as we had the advantage of surprise. We shot down three enemy planes (one flyer escaped by parachute) and attempted to bomb a German pocket battleship. We missed by a few hundred yards, but did considerable damage to the dock area. Some of the other aircrew had better luck at hitting the target.

Not making excuses but we sprang a bad oil leak which made our gun turrets unserviceable, so without their protection we couldn't afford to take a second run. The wireless operator tried desperately to repair the oil leak. His wedding is happening in a couple of weeks and he wanted to come back for it! Our captain/pilot Max is totally cool under pressure and I trust his judgement when it comes to making decisions on the fly. Anyway, he's the boss! After dropping our load he turned for the coast and got us out of there. Halfway across the channel we spotted a damaged Wellington struggling for home on one motor. We accompanied her until our fighters came along to protect her. Then Max put the nose down and headed for the white cliffs of Dover. We landed at an aerodrome in the south to refuel. I had time for a tea in the officers' mess and then lay down on the grass to think of home and other far-off things.

You know that censors prevent me from giving you any more details of the raid, but you'll read about them soon enough. I hope you will realize that I've dramatized the chain of events seriously to make a good story. Don't tell on me! I think this will be the first article written live from inside a bomber during an operation. The next day I was playing golf! It's a strange war, one day dropping bombs from a Lancaster at 8000 ft. over Germany, the next, slicing tiny golf balls onto a green in England.

I love you so much. Remember that family picture we posed for? It's in my pocket wherever I go. Love to all, *Jack*

I Flew into Trouble

Dear Mom and Dad, October 30, 1941

By now you will have received my telegram and perhaps official word from RAF. So you know I am in S. Ireland, or Éire as it is called nowadays (not to be confused with N. Ireland, where I wish I had crashed — at least then I'd be free and back in action). The problem is that Éire is neutral, and you'd think that would be good for us, but it's not, definitely not. I thought they would keep us for a few days while they worked out the papers to repatriate us. Éire is home to the former IRA who, as you know, distrust the Brits whom they blame for 'British Rule' which kept them "prisoner in their own country" for five hundred years. Other neutral countries, like Switzerland, Sweden, and Spain, for example, repatriate downed airmen, but Éire takes prisoners from both sides, Nazis and Allies. They think that's being fair.

They consider that treating us well makes up for keeping us prisoner; e.g., they give us day parole. We're permitted to sign out in the morning after signing an oath to return at night. The Nazis are housed separate from us, and we're not allowed to mingle while on parole, as if we'd want to! So, there are pubs that are known as friendly to the Allies, and pubs that are friendly towards the Nazis, believe it or not. The RAF has signed a covenant with de Valera, the Prime Minister of Éire, pledging that any prisoners who escape during day parole will be returned to the Curragh. That makes my blood boil.

Here's another twist: apparently at night, we're free, nay OBLIGED, to try to escape and return to our duties. Who dreams up these contracts? The Canadian High Commissioner, John D. Kearney, visited and tried to justify the arrangement to us and, believe you me, we all objected strenuously, and then he walked away, promising to return when we had cooled our heels. The guards simply laugh at us when we explain that our ancestors are Irish. "Ha!" they say, "take a spoonful of your own medicine. Your king kept us down, so now we're getting our own back."

You'd probably like to know the series of events that landed me here. First of all, nobody was hurt. We all parachuted safely but I landed in a bog and couldn't move until morning. I hoped to hide in a barn, then walk at night to N. Ireland, to be repatriated. Alas, a mere child spotted me and called to his parents, "Lookit the man!" I walked about 10 miles when someone stopped me and invited me into the Guard house for a 'nice cuppa tae.' Inside were Bobby and the crew sergeants feasting on bacon, eggs, beans and toast, so I helped myself to a plateful. They passed around a bottle of Jameson's so we each took a swig. Shock! It goes down like a hammer in the morning!

Then followed questioning. We gave false names and insisted that our grandparents came from County Clare and supported the Gaelic revival in Boston, but they wouldn't buy it. Meanwhile they fed us more Irish whiskey. Eventually we were allowed to go outside, lie on the lawn and rest in the sun. As I lay on the green, green grass of Ireland looking up at the blue, blue sky, I thought of you and wondered when I would ever see home again.

Bobby and I were hoping to escape (instead of lying in the sun) BUT a crowd of locals had gathered to gape at us. One was a priest, and for some reason, I took offence at him, his being a representative of the Church's values for whom we are fighting this war. Éire wants to keep us prisoner, we who are fighting to protect this very island. It makes no sense! I gave him a large piece of my mind, much to the amusement of the onlookers. They seemed to enjoy hearing a foreigner talking back to a priest. One old lady passed a cap around for donations during my rant!

The reason we were all arrested so promptly is that everyone had seen the explosion from the crash so they were on the lookout for us. Plus, when Bobby sent out the mayday call they all heard it on their short wave radios! We were hardly parachuting in secret even though we crashed at night.

They are afraid the Nazi U-boats, which are lurking in the Irish Sea, will simply swim into their harbours and take over the island. They have the same covenant with the Nazi prisoners, their version of neutrality.

I promise you, I'm going to write a book about this weird situation. Nobody in the Commonwealth would believe it except on the word of an eyewitness. Bobby and I are already making a plan of escape, so don't be surprised if I go missing again. They're not going to shoot us in the back.

I'll need money to buy some civilian clothes, something to fit in with the local scene. Just take it out of my account and cable it to the Canadian High Commission in Dublin. £50 should buy me a nice tweed suit and turtleneck and shoes. If you would knit me a pair or two of your beautiful socks, Mom, I would love that. The ones you sent to England are back there, across the Irish Sea, alas, in my trunk.

I'll write again when I unscramble my head. I did suffer a slight concussion from the ack-ack but it was only momentary. I'm sure there is more to this story. I think about you every day. Love to all, *Jack*

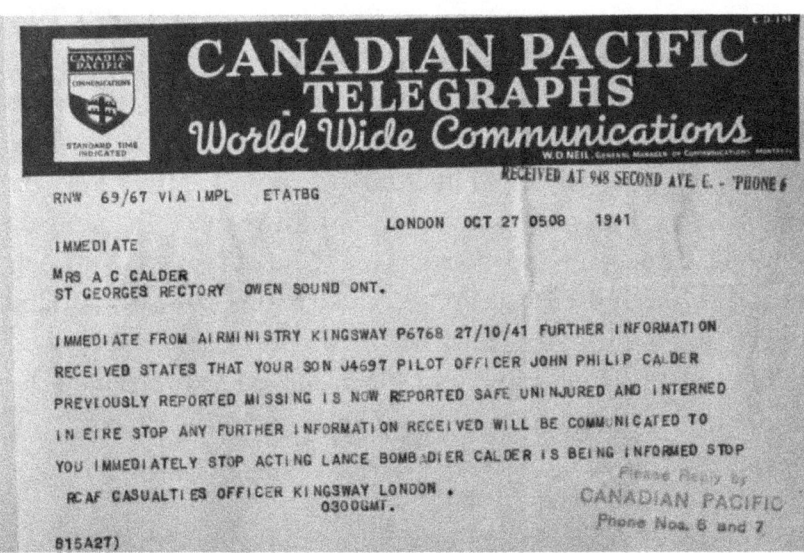

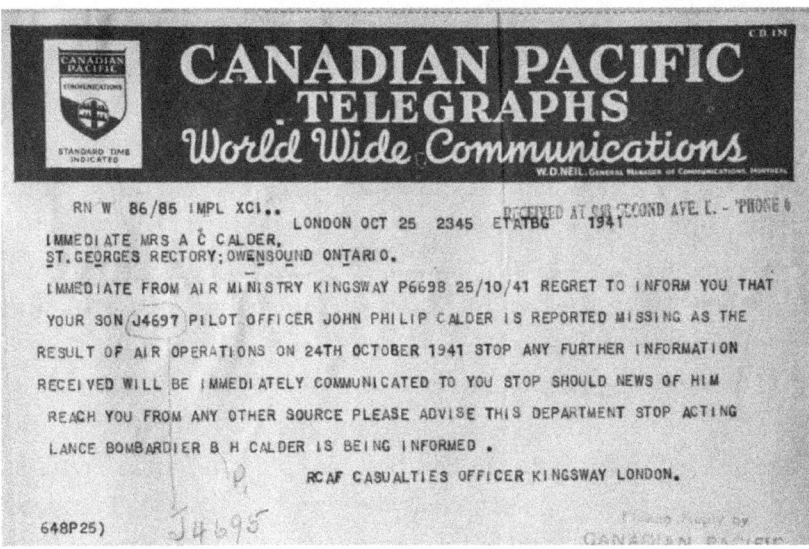

Dear Mom and Dad, October 31, 1941

Éire, cont'd. There's more to the story of how we landed in Éire and what it's like here so far. First of all, we were returning from a mission to Frankfurt. We had been shot at by the anti-aircraft guns and consequently lost our loop antenna (radio direction finder), which meant I was using dead-reckoning. The problem was a thick layer of icing cloud (which causes the aircraft to crash), so we had to fly either above it, where we couldn't see the landmarks, or below it, and be subjected to more flak attacks. Also the weather had changed since we left England and now a strong tailwind blew us off course. When we finally poked through the icing cloud to take a look, we saw land, but was it England, or Ireland? As we came closer we could see lights, so it was definitely not black-out country. Ireland, but was it north or south? Would we be parachuting onto friendly or neutral soil?

We were forced to take our chances because we were running out of fuel. With five minutes of fuel left, the starboard engine cut out, and Bobby ordered the crew to evacuate the aircraft. I lined up the second pilot, rear gunner, and wireless operator at the escape hatch for their first parachute jump and they disappeared one by one. Then it was my turn.

Jumping was easy. The slipstream grabbed my feet and wind caught me in its grasp. I pulled the rip cord; when the chute opened my head was jerked back and I felt as if I were being sawn through. Suddenly the first thing I noticed was the desperate quiet after eight hours of the droning engines and sputtering telephone.

I shouted for Bobby and got no reply. Then I heard the low whirr of our aircraft — a two-engine Wellington, C for Charlie — gliding to her finish. Bob had planned to ditch her in the sea, but now she seemed to be coming around. I learned later that he had headed her out to sea, started to jump and then had seen she was turning inland. He returned to the controls, pointed the machine toward the Atlantic and jumped. The aircraft came around again and finally broke her back in a pasture. If she had ditched in the sea, as planned, no one would have witnessed the crash. We were unlucky in that, but lucky in that I had had time to destroy all our maps, documents, and instruments.

Bobby was unlucky. When he landed in a bog, he revived an old football knee injury, and could barely limp by morning. He was captured quite easily, although he gave nothing away concerning the other crew members. The Garda were laughing at us because we all told different stories. While we were spinning our yarns, what we didn't know was that the locals had heard our mayday call on their wireless radios and had witnessed the crash.

When I had landed in the bog, I had to sit on a little tuft of grass 'til morning because all around me was marsh. I ate a piece of chocolate, thinking what to do. I tore off the insignia and wings from my uniform. Come morning, I hid my parachute. Then as I was walking along before being arrested, cheerily saying hello to everyone I met, trying to blend in, they all knew for a certainty that I was not from around there, despite my red hair and freckles. They were having a good laugh.

The Curragh prison itself is not so bad. It's a row of simple huts, supported by posts. The idea behind hoisting the huts in the air is to prevent tunneling. There goes our first plan of escape! The guards so far are friendly; at least they're not Nazis.

The German prisoners are separate from us, across a high wall. We can hear them, though, especially if they think they've had a victory.

I'm eager to get out on parole, which will happen in a couple of weeks. Then we'll be able to meet the locals and set up some arrangements for our future escape. Apparently we can go to pubs and parties, even dances. There's a golf course nearby, and of course the famous Curragh racetrack. The guards keep telling us about all the local entertainment, as if we really are going to enjoy being guests in their prison. I have to say again, what a stupid arrangement. My first impression of the Irish is that they're given to simple pleasures and a hard luck life of labour. We should be out of here shortly. Love to all, *Jack*

My dear Jack,   **Nov. 2, 1941**

Your mother and I received three telegrams, Oct. 25 from the Air Ministry alerting us that you were missing, and thankfully, another on Oct. 27 informing us that you are "safe, uninjured, and interned in Éire." Those days between the two telegrams we were on our knees! We also received your telegram on Oct. 29, all too brief, my boy, as we are anxious to know details. It is inconceivable that you are actually a POW in Ireland. Canadian Press is doing a good job of covering the story. One piece says it best:

"Irony — or Éireony — remains that Calder and his mates are held prisoners of war by a people who owe their very existence to Britain's RAF and Royal Navy …. De Valera must carry on his nauseating neutrality and treat Jack and others in a similar jam as if they weren't, in the final analysis, the very best friends he has."

Another editor writes: "It is a queer turn of the wheel which finds a Canadian interned in Éire because he was fighting for the British Empire, and incidentally for the rights of all small nations, inside or out."

And this will make you chuckle: "His former desk mates happily cabled word of his safety while aware of his amusement when he hears they had half-finished a story of his being reported missing which read much like an obituary."

Bobby is getting good coverage as well, undoubtedly more in Montreal. I believe you helped to make him famous in that city. I am grateful that you are together now. At least you can lean on each other, and perhaps plot your escape! Your mother has written a note of good cheer to B's mother. Good news is hard to come by lately, so we must celebrate what little we have.

Ah! Just took a break from writing because the mail arrived. One letter from RAF Headquarters in Elsham Wolds listing your personal effects says that the cash found in your trunk or kit bag will be forwarded to the Central Depository, Colnbrook. Do you have an idea how much cash was there? We should keep a record here too. When you escape (!) you won't be able to carry such information with you.

A short note from your commanding officer, O. Godfrey, says: "We are very sorry to lose your son from the squadron as he was our best navigator, but we are all terribly thankful that no harm has come to him."

The wife of your squadron commander, Helen Constantine writes: "We have become great friends both with Jack, and his friend Bobby Keefer … how much we thought of them and how loved they were in the mess …. From every point of view Jack has been a tremendous success — so clever — so cool and brave — and always making a joke about the most difficult things."

The Chaplain writes: "I knew your son very well whilst he was at Elsham …. Perhaps one day we shall see him again at our station as I expect he will do his best to effect an escape!! I should like you to know how much we all liked him at Elsham — he made friends of us all — and his cheerfulness and good humour was a joy to us all …. I am also sure you would be pleased to know that the Sunday before his flight he was present at Holy Communion in our Chapel."

And here's a treat for you: Mrs. Isobel Horner has knitted you a long-sleeved turtleneck sweater which she was saving for Christmas but wants to mail to you now! You lucky boy!

One more note arrived today and that was from Senator Arthur Meighan, just wishing you well.

My hand is aching from writing all that news down, but I thought it would cheer you to know the kind words people are sending us. Keep your spirits up, my son, and don't let those Nazis on the other side of the wall depress you. They're only boys, after all. Much love, *Dad*

Dear Mom,   Nov. 5, 1941

Have you met some new friends in Owen Sound? You see the best in people. Dad always wants us to take a positive view of every parishioner and I sense it is not always easy for you. I've noticed you have a certain way of pursing your lips when you don't agree with Dad.

    Anyway, here I am in Éire, in the Curragh prison for what is looking more and more like a long time. We're hoping for a negotiated release, but there are some airmen who have been here over a year.

    The morning we were arrested I tried to argue variously that we are Canadian but were born in Dublin, that we have American cousins and supported the police strike, that we were greatly interested in the Gaelic revival. I lied about my name (Jackie Fitz-Calder) and Bobby's too (Babby O'Keefer), said we were from "county" Belfast, but the interrogators just seemed to enjoy our fibs as if they were a joke. Then they drove us to the crash site and pointed to the bullet holes in the fuselage, proving that the Wellington crashed on its return from a bombing mission in Europe, an operational flight, not a training exercise. If it had been the latter, we might have been released, but as it stands, we are detained.

At the scene of the wreckage the Irish army seized 1,500 rounds of live ammunition plus two Browning guns from the turrets. They tore the canvas from the frame like skin from an animal carcass. Our rear gunner tried to trade his turtleneck sweater in exchange for his freedom but the guards would not buy it. Instead they drove us in a lorry to the army barracks in Limerick, a two-and-a-half hour trip in a five-ton which tossed us around like mice in a cage. We passed men in suits tilling the fields, women washing clothes in the Shannon River, children playing by their sides. The misty, gentle slopes of the river banks, the birch and willow trees, the friendly faces (of people who hadn't been living in fear of bloody night raids for two years) reminded Bobby and me of the Ottawa valley. We also saw gypsy caravans, tinkers, who are allowed to roam from county to county helping themselves to whatever food they can find, claiming to be dispossessed Irish gentry. When we asked a guard what he knew about the war, he said, "We never had much to do with Europe, that's your concern."

After they gave us a meal, we were informed that we would be taken to the Irish Army's military base southwest of Dublin where we would be held in a camp, the Curragh, under command of a certain Colonel Thomas McNally, and that the diplomatic representative would visit us in due course. Then we drove north, past Tipperary ("It's a long way... ♫"), finally into the heart of county Kildare.

The day of our arrest we were plied with multiple shots of Irish whiskey. After we had slept off the effects, we awoke to another strange new reality. We have free access to a bar in the Curragh, a bar that bills each man on the honour code. Yes, we pour our own drinks and then sign for them in a blue ledger, C for Calder, etc. The Jameson's and Guinness are free!

When Bobby was initially interrogated by McNally he refused to answer any questions, naturally, and furthermore stood tall and asserted, "If we are to be handled as prisoners, we will act like prisoners, and not take advantage of parole." Well, when the rest of us crew heard that our commanding officer had assigned us to a dreary life of staring at five huts surrounded by bales of barbed wire up to twelve feet high, a wall with a huge white G for German painted on it, and a dusty courtyard with a few rocks, we were not well pleased and gave him a hard time. After a few days of that nonsense he changed his mind.

Our first experience on parole was as bizarre as this whole venture into Irish country living. We opted to play golf as the camp links is within sight of the Curragh and Bobby is not only a football and hockey player but also a golf fanatic. So, after signing our pledge to return to prison, we grabbed bicycles from a shed at the camp and rode across the way to the greens. The first surprise was to find that there are no other patrons of the country club, a golfer's dream come true. Reason? Fuel shortage limits the locals' opportunity to drive to the links. The view from the first tee is spectacular. A green panorama stretches out towards large country estates buffered by gorse, heather, and bracken, with no sound but the wind whistling across the plain.

Second surprise was to find sheep littering the greens. No amount of shouting could budge them, even when a ball came whizzing into their midst. I hit one on the head and killed it dead, witnessed its knees buckle in front of my eyes. Our major suggested we haul it off the course to a nearby feed shelter where he happened to find a bucket of red paint, so we painted a large swastika on the unfortunate animal and hoped the farmer would blame the other side. The next day when the farmer sent a complaint to Colonel McNally, he suggested we pay for the sheep. An anonymous envelope of cash found its way to his desk.

Our pay is being transferred to a local branch of the Dublin bank. Bobby bought an old set of golf clubs, and I bought — wait for it — an old typewriter. That's why this letter is the first to be typewritten. Now you don't have to struggle to make out my scrawl.

Mom, I realize our internment would be far worse if we were POWs in Germany. Still, the situation is mighty frustrating. We volunteered to join the RCAF and fight the enemy, not to sit on our duffs in the Curragh. It's annoying that people think we're living on easy street. The British program spent thousands of dollars training each one of us; they need us. Now all that effort is for naught. At the moment I don't see a way out, but we'll stay quiet and observe until we figure out what to do. At least no one is shooting at us, even though the guards do hold real guns and have dogs. They even threaten once in a while to assert their manhood.

Well, my dear mother, I've run out of words for tonight. Hope to hear from you soon. There's so much going on here that's new. I'd love to tell you all about it in person but that will have to wait until after the war. G'night. Love to all, *Jack*

Dear Mom,   Nov. 10, 1941

Your care package arrived and I'm wearing the socks! Thank you, my dear Mother. You are a champion. The jams, sardines, and underwear will all be appreciated in the coming days. There's nothing like a set of Stanfield's best to make a chap feel comfortable in his clothes.

I'm feeling rather melancholy tonight, Mom. I miss flying. On a full moon night, high in the sky, looking down on the world slowly slipping by, I am filled with awe. Flak seen from above is actually quite beautiful, all its colours, red, blue and yellow, streaking high like an upside down waterfall. I feel the tide shifting. Did I tell you that as we were flying home from Germany last time there were people on the ground waving at us with torches? I have moments that I forget I'm in a war, flying a bomber, and just think of the wonder of being suspended in air like a balloon. It's not quiet, but the roar of the four Merlin engines after hours and hours many nights in a row, becomes dull like a train in the distance, a hum like an electric generator. Only when it stops and the rush of quiet assaults one's ears, does one realize how loud the roar was, how majestic.

I miss the officers' mess, the fellowship at breakfast after a mission, the lingo of pilots and navigators and engineers mingling, the swearing, the greetings shouted across the room, the news spilling out of them. I wonder who's missing since I've been gone, who's missing that I don't even know about. I can't wait to get back with the boys and fly ops. I suppose I even miss the danger, the excitement, the thrills, the adrenalin rushes, and the knowledge that we're accomplishing something important. Here in the Curragh we're accomplishing zero, zip, nada. Everything is boring: golf, horse racing, and dancing which should all be fun have no purpose beyond stretching the clock towards another midnight, another parole day gone.

I miss the train station platforms jammed with couples saying good-byes, and train trips packed with servicemen returning from leave, their grim faces thinking of the task before them. Churchill needs every RAF officer and NCO if he is to fulfill his promise to the world: "We shall fight on unconquerable until the curse of Hitler is lifted from the brows of mankind." Thousands of dollars have been spent to train each one of us prisoners and yet we lie idle.

Tell Dad to write a barrage of letters to the diplomatic office in Dublin, to Churchill, to the Canadian High Commissioner. So ends my rant, dear Mother. I know you understand my frustration. I'm unaccustomed to failure. I'm accustomed to action; I'm not a very patient prisoner. We simply must escape. I'm in a great mood, eh. Love to all, *Jack*

Dear Dad,   **Nov. 30, 1941**

Brother Jake surprised me yesterday by dropping in from London for a visit. He'd heard I was grounded at the Curragh and managed to get the weekend off to come over on the ferry. I tell you, Dad, it was so great to see him. He was as flummoxed as Bobby and I are by our internment, especially the parole angle, so we demonstrated by taking him out to a local pub for a proper tell-all. We had to prevent him from tackling a couple of Germans we met in town. He wanted the three of us to take them down, but of course that's one of the rules: no fighting while on day parole. We had a good meal before leaving him for the night. He rented a room in the pub and went back on the ferry early next morning.

I wrote to Mom about our golfing. We've also been going out to the horse races on Sat. night. The racetrack is just across the road from the camp. I've won a few bob; also lost a few bob, so I'm no further ahead. I don't bet too much yet; I'm still getting to know the horses. Don't worry; I won't gamble all my pay. We wager for the fun of it.

You wouldn't believe the wealth of the English landowners. No wonder the Irish hate the Brits. Apparently after William II of Orange won the Battle of the Boyne, many Protestants took over large swaths of land from poor Irish farmers. They stayed and they're still here. We were invited to a big foxhunt, the season's inauguration of the Kildare Hunt Club, held at Ardenaude in Ballymore-Eustace.[i] (That's the way they do the addresses of these huge country estates, the name followed by the county, no street address.) The owner of this particular estate, a stud farm of 650 acres, founded the Irish Sweepstakes in the late 1930s. These aristocrats are called the horse Protestants on account of the flourishing race industry in these parts.

We rode bicycles for at least two hours and passed many estates, beautiful landscapes with tennis courts, carriage houses, stables, small concrete statues, fish ponds, sprawling lawns and lavish country gardens. We had assumed this country to be poor, so it was quite a shock to be invited to a dinner and dance at one of these estates. I had to beg Bobby to go with me; he was determined not to enjoy any of the fruits of parole besides golf and horse racing. He's afraid if he enjoys himself too much he'll lose interest in trying to escape and get back to the horrible business of bombing the hell out of Germany. Instead of that we danced the night away in an expansive ballroom to Jimmy Dunny and his ensemble, a jazz band of sorts, with a brass section from England and a string section from County Claire, playing an oddball collection of American hit tunes (Keefer, 86). The women's ball gowns were exquisite. The daughter of the owner wore a stunning white dress with red ribbons and red shoes. Bobby danced the night with her. I spread my charms around!

In spite of the Irish being almost entirely in favour of neutrality, I've learned that thousands of them have left to join the RAF or the Royal Navy or the work force in UK. ("Curiouser and curiouser," said Alice.) Of course many of them have no political leanings; they need to work for pay.

One item of interest about bike riding: one has to give the right-of-way to the Germans because they ride in large groups abreast. No one can get past them the way they hog the road. Many a local farmer has been forced into the ditch by them and complained to the German embassy in Dublin but they still ride in a cavalcade. You feel as if the cavalry is coming at you, which might be the intent. Some German internees caused a brawl one afternoon with the RAF just outside our camp. Both sides claimed to be on the correct side of the road, and they would have been had they been at home.

I want to hear all about how you're getting along in Owen Sound so I hope you'll have time to write me another one of your wonderful letters. We live for news from home here in the Curragh. Love to all, *Jack*

Dear Mom and Dad,   **Dec. 4, 1941**

How are you both? Thank you for your letters and that wonderful care package. Another pair of socks is much appreciated. The damp of Ireland really seeps into every crevice of exposed skin. What a wonderful surprise to find the turtleneck sweater from Isabel Horner. My favourite colour too, a beautiful teal blue. I shall write her a note to thank her personally. I remember meeting her and her husband many times at Maple Leaf Gardens. The berry jam I remember too. The sardines from Grandpa Calder's factory on Campobello Island are such a treat, and give me a story to share of my ancestors riding the ocean waves in Grandpa's fleet. Also I remember a yarn about my uncles teaching the Roosevelt boys how to sail, is that correct? Remind me of those details. I'd like to tell the lads about it.

Our ranks are swelling here on this fair green isle. On November 30 our first American arrived. His Spitfire fighter was wrecked on a foggy Sunday morning in Moneydarragh, County Donegal. Local people could hear but not see the aircraft flying overhead. Then through the fog they saw a lone figure of a man descending under a parachute and at the same time they heard the crashing sound as his aircraft slammed into the distant countryside. PO Wolfe had been flying escort to a tanker convoy which he had assumed was headed for Galway, Scotland, but which was later confirmed to be heading for Ireland. He was indignant. "What in hell do those assholes need oil for? They're not the ones fighting." Wolfe is determined not to stay "in this dump." He's pretty damn sure the American Embassy will be up to better snuff than the Canadian in terms of repatriating him. We'll see about that.

I don't think Wolfe, the American can be counted on to return after parole; he makes it perfectly clear that he doesn't hold the chit-signing to be legally binding. We've tried to convince him that it's a matter of honour between the RAF and the Dublin government; he argues that his duty is to fight the enemy and he is honour-bound to escape prison by ANY means. We debate these things among ourselves and sometimes the debates become very hot. Bobby and I left for a game of golf to blow off steam.

One officer, Flight Lt. Ward would have been our commander by seniority but has 'special parole' to live off base on a Protestant stud farm with his wife. This arrangement causes some jealousy because he only has to check in every few days with the police hut whereas the rest of us must check in by 2 a.m. every 24 hrs.

Indications are pretty strong that Roosevelt will soon announce America's involvement. If he does, de Valera will follow suit, having a mother born in Manhattan and having been saved by the US from execution by the Brits as IRA. If those dominoes fall, the camp will be closed and we'll all be released. Most of us have packed our bags. We've been celebrating in Naas, Co. Kildare at a hotel called Osberstown House. When we returned the other night we raised a hullabaloo and threw rocks over the wall at the Germans. Sunday evening we went to church and listened to the usual dry sermon by a retired Anglican army chaplain predicting the end of the war.

Two of our officers are Polish. PO Karniewski ditched last March in Dublin Bay where he was rescued and then feted by the Protestant members of the Dublin Yacht Club before being carried off to the Curragh. PO Baranowski crashed in April rather suspiciously in good weather with sixty gallons of gas in his tank.

Then there's the New Zealander, Sub-Lieut. Bruce Girdlestone (Keefer, 90), a volunteer pilot with the Royal Navy, and Maurice Remy, a fighter pilot from the Free French forces who landed in June, famous for having downed a Henkel III in County Waterford. So you can guess, our debates are fairly loud and international in political flavour.

This is the only news worth repeating. I miss you, dear ones, and hold you in my prayers.

Love to all, *Jack*

Dear Jack,   **Dec. 5, 1941**

We are so delighted, my dear boy, that you are safe all in one piece. Such an amazing story we're hearing of your parachute landing and day of arrest. What a tale! We're very proud of you.

I'm enclosing a little story the *Toronto Star* printed that will amuse you. When an older clergyman gets a phone call, that's pretty big news, apparently. I don't mind; ours is a good story for a change.

Foster Hewitt is still doing a great job announcing hockey on Saturday nights. Judge Morley and I usually catch the game — if I have my sermon written, that is. Some other things have changed. There are not many cars roaming the streets these days; we have gas rationing here the same as you do. Bicycles are the chosen mode of transportation (the main street, 2nd Avenue E., is clogged when the collegiate gets out after 4 o'clock).

Your mother and I drove to a farm to spend time with a family who have lost two sons to the war. That time spent together in the car affords us an opportunity to share what's been on our minds. When you do settle down and get married, son, be sure to choose an intelligent woman with whom you enjoy conversation. Don't imagine you're falling in love if she's only pretty and curvaceous. Those attributes are a joy for sure but marriage is a partnership. Your letter about the dance at the hunt club got me thinking. Be careful, my boy. You'd be a good catch for some Irish colleen; you probably look very dashing in your blue uniform. You're old enough now to take a measured approach to romance, and I trust your instincts. Your mother wants grandchildren, for sure, but she can wait until you're home in Canada. Enough fatherly advice!

I find walking has been a great way to familiarize myself with Owen Sound. They have a well-established farmer's market here, which I enjoy. I can usually buy a good chicken for your mother's Sunday dinner. The odd time we'll find one on the back porch in a basket, dropped off by a kindly farmer as token payment for something. In other words, the place is growing on your mother and me. We'll be fine here. With Georgian Bay on the one side and the bluffs on the other, the whole area is picturesque. Mary and Marjorie each have a couple of days off at Christmas and your mother and I can't wait to show them off to the congregation, as well as show them around town.

By the way, your old high school principal, Mr. Sexsmith, sent us a Christmas card again this year, and asked to be remembered to you boys. And the music teacher, Mr. Chamberlain sends his wishes as well. You boys made quite an impression on your teachers, and they pray for you. Someone else is praying for your safe return: remember your old girlfriend Marilyn Simpson? I always liked her. She wrote to your mother inquiring after your health and asked for your address. Expect a letter.

I respect your trying to escape; just don't get shot in the attempt.

Well, your mother is calling me to dinner. I'll write again before Christmas. Try to go to church when you have the opportunity. May God watch over you. Love, *Dad*.

OVERJOYED SON SAFE DAD DOESN'T PREACH

Rev. A. C. Calder Had Worried on Hearing Son, Jack, Missing

As Rev. A. C. Calder, of Owen Sound conducted two morning services in his church there Sunday morning, his mind strayed often from his text. As he had passed through a nearly-sleepless (sic) night, he thought constantly of a telegram he had received late Saturday telling him that his son, P.O. Jack Calder, RCAF, was "missing after air operations."

Sunday night, Mr. Calder did not preach. For at 5:30 p.m. yesterday he received a telephone call informing him his son was interned in Éire. The reaction was too great for him to go on with the service.

"I stayed home with my wife, and Judge (E. W.) Morley took the service," he told *The Star* by telephone today. "The relief was immense, the reaction great."

"For about 22 hours I thought my son was missing," he continued. "Then came a telephone call from Mr. (A. E.) Fulford of *The Canadian Press*, telling us he was safe. It is the kind of thing that happens only once in a lifetime. Once is enough!"

While he spoke to *The Star*, he excused himself momentarily. Someone was at the door. It was a cablegram from the RCAF casualties office, England. Mr. Calder returned to the telephone.

"This makes it official," he said, and read the cable:

"Further information received states your son, Pilot Officer Jack Philip Calder, previously reported missing is reported safe, interned in Éire," he read.

P. O. Calder, former Canadian newspaperman, wrote a by-lined story last August on a raid on the Gneisenau. Calder was sports writer and Ontario editor in the Toronto and Montreal bureaus of the Canadian Press. He left the CP 18 months ago. A brother is an acting bombardier in the Canadian army in Britain.

Dear Dad,   Dec. 10, 1941

The Americans have finally entered the war. I'm sorry for their losses at Pearl Harbour, but I must confess we were celebrating here in the Curragh (probably the only ones in the Allied world to be partying the night of Dec. 8th). We believe it means de V. will have to close the camp and we can go back to our duties. Strange to tell, no one here except me had ever heard of Pearl

Harbour. I had to explain where it is and what the significance of the attack could mean for the future of the war.

We all poured in to Naas, the village where the Osberstown House Hotel is located, to hoist a few brew. The owners of the establishment, Jim and Tom, are becoming great pals of Bobby and me. Also we met Josephine, the bar maid, fluent in 3 languages, English, Irish, and German. It doesn't hurt to have friends on the outside (Keefer, 98).

Again when we returned to camp we threw rocks over the wall at the Germans. Boyish pranks, I know, but such fun at 2 a.m.

When Jake visited he told us stories of POWs who had escaped and could write their own ticket and if we are released, or escape (whichever comes first) we hope to be able to write our own ticket; i.e., the RAF will be so glad to see us we can choose where we want to serve. Of course Bobby and I will happily go back to Squadron 103, if they'll have us.

Jake will be exporting this letter from prison and he'll send it to you from London, so I can speak freely.

Last June, one fellow, Paul Mayhew, a former prisoner at the Curragh, escaped over the wall with two others. His father is an English diplomat who enlisted the help of MI9, the British intelligence agency. They sent a few agents to cut the wire and help the prisoners escape to the North. The escape was successful but the Irish objected, so the RAF outlawed any similar attempts in future.

Bobby and I took our first Dublin day parole. We toured the city — Leinster House, Trinity College, St. Stephen's Green, Abbey Theatre, Customs House, College Green, and finally the General Post Office, the scene of the great republican uprising of 1916. Afterward we enjoyed dinner at a favourite pub of the IRA called Jammet's. It came to light that there is another Curragh camp, for IRA members, a mile down the road from ours, but whose prisoners do not enjoy parole. They're lucky if they get food and water. Even though de V. is former IRA, he is not appreciated now because of his treatment of his former colleagues, so they will do anything to embarrass him, even help us. If we escape the camp confines on our own, we might be able to count on IRA sympathizers to hide us while we sneak our way north to Belfast. From there we will be repatriated to Britain. Remy, the Frenchman, accompanied us to dinner and pointed out a woman named May, IRA, who might be sympathetic and help us to hide out. We'll bide our time (Keefer, 104).

It would be politically advantageous for the IRA to help prisoners escape and embarrass de V. because then he might lose the next election and the IRA could swoop in and take over the reins.

Better not tell Mom that we might be getting in bed with the IRA. I don't care to add to her worries. There will be time for telling tales after we escape. And don't you be worrying either; I don't want to hear of any more sleepless nights. Carry on as if nothing is afoot. Remember, no one has been shot while escaping. The worst that can happen is they'll escort us back to camp. Love you, Dad. *Jack*

Dear Mom and Dad,   Dec. 18, 1941

One week until Christmas. Another care package arrived. Mother, you're spoiling me. The cookies are delicious, surprising considering the rationing in Canada. I can't believe you were able to buy a chocolate bar. No matter; thank you for thinking of me. I wish I had something to send you both. I'll make it up to you when I come home and spoil you rotten.

Two more crashes brought new prisoners to the Curragh. On the 16th of December in Clogher, Co. Donegal, a Spitfire crashed and another Canadian arrived, Sergeant Duncan Fowler. Difficulties with his aircraft caused Fowler to make a pancake landing on a strand near Clogher. He was promptly arrested by a member of the LDF (Land Defense Force) and transported to the Curragh.

Again on the 16th a Sunderland Flying Boat crashed into Galway Bay. On returning from a patrol in the Atlantic the aircraft was running low on fuel. The pilot tried to put the sea plane down in Galway Bay, but on contact with the water the outer engine port wing broke off and the aircraft began to list and sink. The pilot ordered the crew to abandon the plane. Seven of its crew perished in the sea but two survived. The pilot, Flight Lt. Grant Fleming, DFC, from Calgary, swam for two hours, three miles to shore in the frigid waters of the N. Atlantic (Keefer, 105). Sergeant Jimmy Masterson, an Olympic swimmer from Perth was the only other to survive. They were given warm blankets and a change of clothes before being transported to join our gang of prisoners. (Any Allied or German air crew found within three miles of the Republic of Ireland's coast are arrested.)

The new arrivals have to spend a couple of weeks at the Curragh before their privilege of day parole begins, as did we. The guards expect us to be planning an escape, especially now that we have reinforcements.

It's too bad that all of us landed in this sorry place, but we are very glad to hear news of the boys back in the UK. We had a grand night of drinking and story-telling. Of course Fleming and Masterson were subdued because of the loss of their crew. Fleming was particularly downcast; as the pilot he felt responsible. We tried to make the best of things by filling them in on the peculiarities of day parole. We even talked about the possibilities of escape, although being surrounded by two 10' rolls of barbed wire is not encouraging.

News flash from the Curragh: That American I told you about, Wolfe, did not return from parole, just as he promised. Long story short, he signed out; when he came back, the guard was not at his post, so he signed in, out, and in again. Then the police just waved him past to go for a nightcap with a visiting friend because he had already spoken to them. In effect, he was signed in at camp when he was actually out of camp. He took a bus to Dublin and from there a train to Belfast. However, the RAF did not respect his ruse de guerre; the diplomats descended on camp and informed all of us that Wolfe would be disciplined in a formal inquiry, and that further attempts to escape by such means would be met with strict measures, possibly the cancellation of parole for all. It is the spirit of the law, not the letter, which they want us to honour, our word as officers of the RAF (Keefer, 107–108). I argued in front of the whole audience that it is our duty as POW to escape by any means, but was shut down by not only the Canadian High Commissioner but also the wing commander, who were both in attendance. Wolfe returned to camp a chastened man.

You will be receiving this letter before Christmas, so I want to wish you both a joyous holiday. I am safe. Phil is safe. Jake is safe. The girls are busy and happy. I can imagine the church all decorated and the choir rehearsing special music of the season. I hope you have unpacked the Christmas decorations and will dress up the new rectory and have friends over to celebrate. Judge Morley will no doubt be first on the list. Say hello and Merry Christmas from me. The staff is promising to serve us a proper Christmas dinner in the Curragh, and remember, Jameson's and Guinness are free here. I can promise you that we will be jolly, even while missing home. Love to all, *Jack*

Part Two

1942

Dear Jack,   Jan. 4, 1942

How wonderful to receive your recent letters and know that you are safe, even though interned. Happy New Year, dear boy, and may1942 be a new page in your life, contentment, fulfillment of your dream of writing a book. Now you have a typewriter and time, what gifts. I know you will apply yourself with the energy and devotion equal to your reputation as a journalist. Sports writing has taught you how to tell a story, so I think you can make sense of even Irish neutrality. Are you seeing any Gaelic football matches?

    Mary and Marjorie were here for two days each, one being Christmas day. We really enjoyed singing the hymns together in church. Your father gave a very uplifting sermon; I am proud of him. I think the fact that you are safe really put the wind under his wings. Mary absolutely loves her nursing training, especially the maternity ward. The joy of new life raises her spirits. Marjorie is happy in her job at CP and is eager for you to come home and join her in the Toronto office. I drove your father and the girls around town and environs for the tour of our new home. They miss Goderich, of course, but like the look of Owen Sound. A clergyman's life means moving usually every five years, so we were very fortunate to have fifteen years in Chatham and six years in Goderich while you children were growing up.

Judge and Mrs. Morley had some excitement over the holidays. Their son Lawrence came home on leave. They enjoyed five days together before they had to drive him back to Toronto. Bobby's mother visited them from Montreal. Of course, the local rag printed the news; I've included the clipping. You can add it to your wall of cheerful epithets.

Here's another item of interest from *The Owen Sound Comet*. I have learned that Owen Sound has a Polish training camp. Apparently Polish men are being trained in our new armoury. The officers are housed in private homes and the NCOs in a renovated factory. I first learned of their presence when a host, who is billeting a couple of Poles, introduced your father to them after church.

Now that Christmas and New Year are over, the excitement is past, and we must settle down to the practicalities of living in Owen Sound. I absolutely must finish unpacking! Your father and Judge Morley have purchased season's tickets to the hockey games so they will be occupied on Sat. nights until nine o'clock. Mrs. M. and I will have tea and a chat until they come back; then we'll play a few hands of bridge together.

The parishioners here are quite friendly and we're enjoying getting to know the ropes at St. George's. Each parish has its own ways so we're still in the listening stage. Changes can come later, as your father knows well enough! I try to keep a tight hold on the reins in case he runs ahead too fast. You know what he's like when he gets the bit between his teeth.

Sleep well and dream of peace for all. Love, Mom xo

> Sub-Lieutenant Lawrence Morley, R.C.N., spent New Year's leave with his parents, Judge and Mrs. Morley, and has returned to duty. Judge and Mrs. Morley motored to Toronto with their son. Mrs. Keefer of Montreal, who was a guest at the home during the holidays, has returned to Montreal. Mrs. Keefer's son is interned in Éire with Pilot Officer Jack Calder.

A camp to train officers and fighting men of Polish descent exists in the centre of Owen Sound.

Lieutenant Grzelczyk said, "So far away from our home country — Polish soldiers are being trained here on Canadian soil and eventually they will join our forces."

Officers are invited to live in private homes, while fighting men are barracked in a renovated factory on 14th Street West.

The "Stonehenge" home of early pharmacist Stephen J. Parker was renovated by a Toronto Polish Association to become Owen Sound's first armoury. It stands on the northeast corner of 10th Street and 2nd Avenue West.

"It is a fully outfitted Officers' Mess, including an updated kitchen, generous library, sitting room complete with a grand piano, where the Polish officers entertain their hosts and dignitaries with music and song."

The city held a banquet for the Poles to honour them. Soldiers are invited to Sunday dinners after church and synagogue services. Dances are held in the old city hall ballroom.

"Skiing and swimming picnics revitalize the Polish men, who return this hospitality by giving music and singing concerts. Their presence in Owen Sound lifts the cultural standards of the city, when the men click their heels and bow to kiss the ladies' hands," Grzelczyk said.

The Polish officers, instructors, airmen, sailors and soldiers are trained in Kosciuszko Camp in Owen Sound.

"Glory to the Heroes."

Dear Mom and Dad,   Jan. 5, 1942

Another year begins. Happy New Year, my dear Mom and Dad! May 1942 bring peace and a return to normalcy. I have been very happy of late. Thank you for the wonderful care package. I must have the most pampered feet in camp. Your socks are so beautifully knitted, Mom, and the wool so soft yet strong. The matching scarf will keep me warm during the damp winter days. Bobby and I enjoyed the salmon and tinned milk one evening on toast. What a treat! The photographs of Mary and Marjorie I will keep in my wallet. Tell them how pleased I am to receive them. Also I loved their letters and will settle down to reply to each of them very soon. They both sound happy and I am glad for them. The home-made Christmas cards really mean a lot to me. They are pinned on my wall where I see them every day and they warm my heart.

Since Wolfe returned, his formal inquiry was held (Keefer, 110). I must say, the English treated him rather badly. They forced him to write a report, then used it against him, and ignored what the American minister concluded. In the end, most of us sided with him. Our hopes for immediate release are dashed.

Fleming and Girdlestone, two officers I told you about who landed here before Christmas, are housed in the hut next door to ours; we've been hanging out together on trips to Dublin. They are fine fellows and we're becoming good friends. We went back to Jammet's, the IRA pub, and were introduced to May, whom I mentioned before. She agreed to help us should we escape the Curragh.

New Year's turned into a very jolly occasion. Bobby and I attended the Harrier's Ball at Osberstown, the highlight of the hunt season in Co. Kildare. (The Curragh Grandstand hosts the thoroughbreds; Osberstown hosts the hunts and point-to-points.) Bobby and Susan introduced me to her friend, Ann Mitchell, of Ballymore Eustache, a WAAF, home for the holidays from England. Her father is president of the Kildare Hunt Club. Susan wore a stunning long, white lace gown and red elbow-length gloves. Ann looked gorgeous in a two-tone blue gown of silk and taffeta, I think. It swished when she walked and danced. Memorable! Susan wanted to know what Bobby's plans are after the war. Does he have to go back to

Canada? Does he think Ireland a beautiful country? A wonderful place to raise his children? (Keefer, 74).

At that point Bobby excused himself and disappeared. I later learned he had gone to the bar downstairs where he suddenly met a German. Josephine, the blonde bartender, tri-langue, served each of them in turn. The German, Neymeyr, became very friendly, even suggesting that the two of them could end the war right then and there by shaking hands and calling a truce. When Bobby hesitated Neymeyr accused him of having no courage and ordered a bottle of Schnapps. "We will see what we can do about this problem of no courage," he said. "No, we won't," Bobby replied and backed off. On his way back to Susan, he ran into Covington, from the Curragh, who informed him that Neymeyr is a spy who always pretends to be drunk in order to elicit info. The adventure continues.

After the high points of Christmas and New Year's, we've settled into the dreary prospect of winter in the Curragh. The weather is damp and cold. We do have snow though, so at least the countryside looks pretty again.

I've been trying to wrestle some sense out of Irish neutrality for a couple of articles I'm writing. I am gleaning information bit by bit, interviewing members of the gentry, the diplomats, Colonel McNally, even the guards and policemen. Each time I leave on parole I have more chances to talk to people. Everyone has an opinion, and the views don't match up. I'll have to create a sort of balance sheet if I want to write objectively.

A sideline in my research has been former escape attempts. One man, Covington, British, who has been here the longest, has made five attempts. In the end, none was successful, but at least each time he gained information, which we can use to form a strategy for another attempt; for example, there are no censors at work in this camp, so far at least.

The guards are former IRA, many of whom lived here themselves, so they know all the tricks. One thing we can be sure of: they won't shoot us, at least not with real bullets. It would cause too much of a political uproar for de V. All Covington ever experienced was being arrested and returned to camp. One time they shot at his head with rubber bullets. No harm done.

Another time a local widow baked him a cake with a message inside: come to this address, blah blah (full description of her house). A guard ate the cake and found the message. Even if Covington had gone to her house, the LDF would have found him immediately. Apparently she is a bit dotty and has sent several cakes before.

We need a safe house that is discreet with people intelligent enough to hide us for several days until we can make our way to the North. We'll disguise as gypsies or ride on a farm cart or something unlikely to draw suspicion of the police who are always roaming the country roads. We will have to keep our mouths shut so they don't detect our accent. That will be my challenge, with my proclivity for attracting attention with my mouth!

I have been reading a lot too — William Yeats, George Bernard Shaw, about the Horse Protestants and the General Post Office uprising in 1916, everything I can get my hands on. Colonel McNally has been very generous with his library and frequently leaves books on my bed that he recommends. Such is life at the moment.

G'night, dear ones. Love to all, *Jack* (Keefer, *Grounded in Eire*)

Dear Jack,   **Jan. 14, 1942**

Well, at last, here I am. So you've landed yourself in prison. Hope the guards are treating you with respect!

You'll never guess — I'm working in the accounting department. Very promising, eh. I. I was scrounging around the archives of CP when I came across this little gem:

> Did you ever hear of a goalie scoring a goal? It happened in 1905.

Do you have any great anecdotes you can feed me?

I'm loving life at the CP. We're a really tight gang, lots of parties. We don't have enough men to go around but we have a good time anyway. You never actually told me how much fun you had on the job. There are a lot of women here who probably know you, if not for real, then by reputation, so you might as well spill the beans. If you have free Guinness and Jameson's in that camp of yours, I guess it's party central all day long.

Mary and I visited Mom and Dad for a couple of days over Christmas. The rectory at St. George's, Owen Sound is not what I would call home, but the furniture is the same as we had at St. George's, Goderich. It felt a bit strange to see it placed in different rooms. The town is another Scottish enclave. Dad's in his element with a new audience for his sermons. Mom is still trying to figure out where she fits in; the women of the parish have things pretty well in hand. That's good. I'd like to see her reach into the community and try something new. I think she's ready for a challenge now that her brood have all flown the coop.

I hope the Irish are not torturing you and you're just not telling Mom and Dad. If so, send word via Jake and we'll mobilize a protest on this side of the pond. I worry about you — maybe acting too proud or too manly or just too damn brave. If anyone is pulling out your toenails, let me know.

On the other hand, when you get out of there and come home on leave, bring some handsome airmen in blue uniforms with you, will you?

CB sends his best per usual. Lots of love, *Marjorie*

Dear Jack, Jan. 31, 1942

I hope you are faring well this winter in the damp cold of Ireland. We are enjoying our first beautiful winter in Owen Sound. There is more snow than in Goderich. People are outside enjoying all manner of winter sports; cross country skiing and snowshoeing are popular with the younger parishioners. Hockey on ponds and small lakes is still embraced since many of the local arenas are closed; most of the male athletes have joined the troops overseas and there's no money to maintain indoor ice. Sewing team uniforms has transformed into sewing military uniforms.

It's possible that the Collingwood Shipyards will get the contract to build an escort ship for the Royal Navy. Winston Churchill has ordered a fleet of modified corvettes, each named after the community that built her. The corvette class is small, based on a whaling ship design. This one, built in Collingwood, will be called HMCS Owen Sound. It will be launched in the spring of 1943. Isn't that grand? I am happy to hear that those of us at home waiting out the war can contribute something that physical. I've written a letter to the manager of the shipyard, who happens to be Anglican, to ask if I might be invited to the commissioning ceremony. Bold and brash as ever! I doubt if a clergyman will hold much sway, but you never know. It can't hurt to ask. I must confess to being excited by this project.

Controversy is heating up leading to the possibility of a plebiscite on the question of conscription. Most English-Canadians are in favour, while most French-Canadians are not, so it could be a very divisive issue. PM King vs that idiot Godbout (Premier of PQ) are at it tooth and nail with press releases and arguments in both houses; the sides are lining up in the debate.

On January 16, Prince Arthur, Duke of Connaught and Strathearn, 10th Governor General of Canada, died. As a proud Scot, I'm not particularly a monarchist, so I don't normally notice the GG activities or care; however, it will be interesting to see who is chosen to replace Prince Arthur. The appointment is supposed to be non-partisan, but to the astute eye, there's always a whiff of politics involved. The cartoonists will tell the tale.

I've been studying about POWs in Canada. Apparently there are a number of camps, although they are kept rather hush

hush. A farmer near here confided to me that several German men have been loaned to him to work on his farm as his usual help have signed up for the war effort. They are good workers and have settled into the life pretty well; although in the beginning they were restless. One of them even ran away, but he returned after one night in the woods because he was confronted by a bear. Isn't that astounding! You have to love life in Canada.

All POWs are protected by the conditions of the Geneva Convention. Mr. King claims that our prisoners are treated better than average and many times better than Canadian troops in German camps. They are guarded by the Veterans Guard of Canada, mostly men who have been soldiers during WWI. It is believed by some that the lenient treatment has already foiled many escape attempts before they even started. Some say, "You couldn't pay them to escape!"

The enclosed clipping was mailed to me by a colleague in Oshawa. The point of this article seems to be to humanize the enemy. I asked your mother if she would have allowed German POWs to hold Baby Philip if we had lived in similar circumstances. Her reply: "Of course, as long as they didn't have weapons." I objected: "But they could have strangled the Lambert child with their bare hands." "In that case the mother would have said no when she looked into their eyes. A mother would know."

I think we should have one Sunday a year that women preach instead of men. Oh what secrets would be revealed! Your mother lets me toot my horn and I am very grateful that she does; she keeps the peace in our house, but I want to encourage her to speak up more often. She's a wise woman.

Jack, my advice to you is to remember that if you escape you will, odds-on, be caught again, so spend as much time securing safe houses as you spend on the escape plan itself. Good luck, my boy. Love, *Dad*

The sleepy town of Bowmanville received a wakeup call when a former school for wayward boys became a camp for over 800 of the highest ranking officers of the Reich. Camp 30 has two General lieutenants, one General major and a U-boat corvette commander in residence. The latter has been awarded a "Knight's Cross with Oak Leaves and Swords" for having sunk more Allied tonnage than any other U-boat commander. The POWs predominantly maintain themselves within their camps, cooking and cleaning for themselves and they are only lightly supervised by the Canadian Veterans Guard. Their presence, however, is felt in neighbouring communities when they are allowed to farm or swim or even work in local businesses.

Many of the worst Nazis were sent to the former TB sanatorium at Gravenhurst. When the citizens of Gravenhurst saw uniformed German officers with medals gleaming on their chests marching their jackboots in formation through town from the rail station to the POW camp, the war hit the home front with a wallop.

A group of POWs lived within 100 yards of the Lambert family. Fern Lambert recalled the arrival of the prisoners whose imminent presence had aroused curiosity, fear and hatred among the local population. "Our oldest daughter was old enough to realize that they were the enemy, and ran in crying, 'The Germans are coming, the Germans are coming!'"

Baby Lambert, outside on a blanket, halted the procession of enemy aliens in their tracks. The homesick men sent forward an English speaking delegate to ask permission to hold the infant. Mrs. Lambert reluctantly agreed on the condition that the baby be returned to her if she started to cry. Baby Lambert did not cry. She loved the attention as the men gently passed her from arm to arm.

Some of these POWs work in a factory. A few even managed to disguise the red circle and red stripe on their uniforms to slip into town to see a movie.

Dear Mom and Dad,   **Feb. 11, 1942**

Well, the grand scheme came to fruition. On the night of Feb. 8–9 our escape plan was activated. All thirty-one of us were involved, including the NCOs. Everyone took parole as usual to avoid arousing suspicion. The day previous, a wire cutter was smuggled into camp in a golf bag. Bobby spent the entire day in the bicycle shed assembling a ladder made out of shower curtain rods, cable for the rungs, and some used marine shackles. It was fashioned in two sections, first to scale the ten-foot-high wall, and second, a bridge to get us over the top of a four-foot wide bank of barbed wire. From there we would jump and parachute-roll to the ground, then run like the devil in different directions, each to our preplanned safe houses.

    Bobby, who used to work as a lineman for Bell during his summers at McGill, would use the wire cutters to snip an opening in the first wall of barbed wire. After we squeezed through the hole, the ladder would be thrown up against the second wall and we would climb one by one over the top and away.

    Wolfe, the American, and Sgt. Virtue were assigned to arrive back from parole at 10 o'clock. I was to shout, "Lock up the Yankee swine!" while those two tackled the guard, gagged and tied him. At my signal, everyone would run to the cycle shed, which was out of view of the guard towers. From there we had a quick dash to the first barrier. Flash bombs and smoke canisters began exploding in the opposite corner of the compound, distracting the guards in the towers. Everything was going peachy keen, when, incredibly, the ladder collapsed just as Covington and I were crossing the bridge section. The rusted marine shackles retrieved from the waste bin of the Dublin Yacht Club had failed us, and we toppled down onto the lads below.

    Meanwhile Bobby and four others had jumped to freedom; however, Webster was caught by the guards who began beating him with their clubs. Bobby ran back to Webster's defence and Fleming joined him. Then they made a second break for freedom. Bobby's football tactics served him well as he faked and dodged his way past the guards and down the road. At the main gate, a guard exited the duty hut wielding a fire shovel which he swung at Bobby, sending him head over heels to the ground. He was restrained and led back to the barbed wire. Fleming, by this time, was being clubbed viciously by another guard, named Kelly (who spoke German and who nobody liked). Bobby broke lose, and helped Fleming, then those two began beating up Kelly. A general mêlée broke loose with lots of cursing and swearing and anti-British insults flying.

When everything was nearly all over, some soldiers showed up, opening and closing the chambers of their Enfields at us, but didn't fire. Another indication that they have been ordered not to fire on us. Important information for the future.

Our German neighbours were cheering for the guards and throwing rocks over the dividing wall, the same rocks we had thrown at them a few weeks ago.

End of story: nobody escaped (Keefer, 140–45). Three were sent to hospital where they again made a run for it but were recaptured. So ends a disappointing finish to weeks of planning and preparations. We each had to submit separate accounts of events for Col. McNally. To top it all off, our day parole is cancelled.

I'll be able to catch up on my letter-writing. Now you know why I haven't written much since Christmas. I didn't want to spill the beans. Well, we've learned from our mistakes and live to escape another day.

Sleep well, dear ones. One day I'll send you a cable from UK. Love to all, *Jack*

Dear Jack,   **Feb. 14, 1942**

Today being Valentine's Day I am determined to write a letter to each of my children. Your father might be my Valentine, but you children are the loves of my life. Now that you are so far away I find myself rudderless. It gives me great comfort to know that you are happy, have good friends, and a purpose in life. Enough sentimentality!

I've been unpacking the many boxes from the spare room. I came across your high school year book and couldn't resist flipping through the pages. There you are with the editorial staff looking very serious. And a few pages later, there you are with your rugby team looking very athletic. And a few pages later, there you are with 'Jake and his Gravediggers' looking totally comical. (I didn't realize that you and Jake were the only two boys wearing V-neck sweaters while all the others have suit jackets.) Remember how you used to play on the radio on Friday afternoons?

I think the name of the band was intended to poke fun at your dad, and the surprising thing is that he never minded. You children are his pride and joy. Even though he doesn't say it, you can trust me; I know it to be true. When you children were still at home and your dad and I were getting ready for sleep we would often giggle about some prank that you lot had hatched.

Did you know that Wilbur Sexsmith and I are on first name basis? "Agnes, it's my duty to inform you, blah, blah, blah." "Well, Wilbur, do what you have to do. Archie and I will support you." He's retired now, but he was a wonderful principal. He never took your pranks too seriously because you brought honour to the school. Your awards for spelling and your work on the year book, as well as the rugby team, helped disarm any frustration he might have felt. To be honest, he admired your spunk. He could see your talent emerging.

Mrs. Morley and I are becoming friends. She has one visage for the public and another for her intimate circle. She is very astute at evaluating people and has given me the benefit of her years observing Owen Sound. Of course she has the advantage of being married to a judge and therefore being invited into all sorts of homes and public events. She sees the best and worst of a small town and knows all the main players. Actually she cracks me up with her wry sense of humour. You would love her as your quick wit could match hers. You two would get along like a house on fire.

Here's news: the next time Bobby's mother comes to visit from Ottawa, probably at Easter, I am promised a cup of tea and a chat with the dear lady. I wager I will take to her. Warn Bobby that he will likely feel embarrassed while I'm being told tales of his wild and reckless youth. People's ears burn if they're being talked about, even across the miles. I'm not saying what I will share with her! That last news clipping I sent you got her place of residence wrong: she never lived in Montreal, as Bobby did; she lived in Rockcliffe, a posh suburb of Ottawa.

In the evenings your father and I listen to Lowell Thomas read the news, and afterward we hear Jack Benny. Could anyone be funnier? I'm doing the dishes and laughing my head off. When I'm finished, we sit in the living room. I knit and your father pretends to read the paper while he smokes his pipe. Soon he lays it down to enjoy the programme. Do you boys have access to a radio? Can you follow the news or is it censored?

Dad joins me in sending our love. I know you will be careful if you escape. For now I will rest in the knowledge that you are safe. You tell that Sergeant Kelly I'll knock his block off if he beats you again. All my love, *Mom xo*

Dear Dad and Mom,   **Mar. 15, 1942**

Since the failed escape, Feb. 9th. I've recovered from my bruises, both external and internal. Sergeant Kelly landed a few blows with his baton — nothing serious. My pride is hurt more than anything.

The Irish presses are still boasting. Headlines like: NINE BRITISH INTERNEES ESCAPE IN ÉIRE, THREE RETAKEN and ANOTHER INTERNEE RECAPTURED, etc., etc., ad nauseum.

We have one success story to report. Sgt. Webster has escaped. Fortunately for Webster his parole form was filed beside Wolfe's and the duty Captain at the parole hut cancelled the wrong form. Webster was therefore out on parole while he was mistakenly recorded as being in camp. We found his pilot, Brady, who rushed into the village, located Webster in a pub, delivered the cancelled form, and sent him on his way north with a £5 note (Keefer, 167).

Do you remember my telling you about a girl I danced with on New Year's Eve, Ann Mitchell? She's a WAAF so she's leaving for the UK at the end of summer, but in the meantime we've been seeing each other. There's a group of eight of us who socialize together on parole. Her father, Major Mitchell, invited me for drinks at Osberstown (Keefer, 78). He's quite a fine chap. I think you'd like him. He's one of the Horse Protestants who owns a large estate and quite a few thoroughbreds. He's totally wound up with the racing industry. I think he would hide me if I escaped and needed a safe house until I could make my way north. He also invited Bobby and me to a game of golf at Bray, in Wicklow. It's right along the coast of the Irish Sea and features beautiful views in all directions.

Similarly, over Christmas Bobby and I were invited to Major O'Sullivan's for dinner. He is a retired British Army Officer, well connected, who owns a large estate in Foxrock, overlooking Dublin Bay. He offered to help us and if he did it is unlikely the RAF would send us back to the Curragh. First, we have to escape.

I've been trying to figure out why the response of the guards to our escape attempt was so vicious, so angry. Perhaps part of the reason is the disparity between our food rations and theirs. Whereas we are served beef every day, they are living on soup and potatoes. Their children are scrounging for coal behind the trains. The internees on full RAF pay make double what the guards earn. Then there's the antagonism toward the Horse Protestants who ate up all the best land in the south of Ireland. We fraternize with them, so like them, we are hated. Also there is the Irish Catholics' religious affinity with the Germans. De V. not only compared himself to Hitler, he also actually refused

Chamberlain and Churchill's offers of a united Ireland in exchange for joining the Allied cause.

Irish neutrality is a mystery, very complicated. Why would the Irish government allow Herr Hempel, the German ambassador, to fly the swastika over his residence in Dublin, while denying Sir John Maffey, the British representative, the right to fly the Union Jack over his? What's neutral about that arrangement?

De V. is not a big fan of the press. It has come to my attention that G2, the intelligence arm of the Irish army, is checking my mail in and out, steaming open my envelopes and copy-typing my telegrams. Here's the reason: the Canadian high commissioner, Mr. Kearney, has discovered that I wrote the article, "I Flew into Trouble," about our crash landing and internment that *Maclean's* magazine wants to publish. Get this: he's not angry about it; he just wants to know in advance if I plan to write anything more about Irish politics.

By the way, if you hear or read any rumours that we're going to movies with the Germans, attending church with them or any other dang thing, know that they aren't true. We're not allowed to fraternize outside camp at all, ever, nor would we want to.

Good news to go along with the clipping enclosed. The U-26 submarine was depth-charged off the northwestern coast of Ireland. I'm not sure how long ago this happened but we're just hearing about it.

A funny thing happened last night. I was joking around, trading insults with the guard on duty at the parole hut. His rejoinder was: "How can you live in a country that's all Indians and bush?" I think he was half serious. Enjoy your bannock. Love to all, *Jack*

U-BOAT LANDS SHIPWRECKED CREW IN IRELAND

After torpedoing the Greek steamer "Diamentis" 4990 tons, off Land's End on Tuesday, October 3, 1939, the U 35 slipped away into the night.

A German submarine rescued the crew of 28 from the sea and took the men aboard the U-Boat! There they stayed for 36 hours while the undersea craft sought a place on the Irish coast to land them. Finally the ship's crew was set down in a desolate region near Dingle. They were ferried to shore in a collapsible boat. The submarine exchanged greetings with persons on land, then moved from the coast and started to submerge before Civic Guards on patrol duty had time to detain it.

The Spanish River Pulp and Paper Co. Mill, in Canada, converted to Camp 21, received most of the 38 crew members of captured U 35. The actions of these enemy aliens earned them the cover of LIFE magazine October 16, 1939.

"LIFE'S COVER: The German submarine U 35, shown on the cover, distinguished itself last week by bagging a Greek steamer and bringing the survivors to the Irish shore. It is a 500-tonner built three years ago at Krupp's Germania yards at Kiel and flies the Nazi war flag with a red field. It is painted gray on the sides to blend with the sky and black on top to blend with the water when submerged."

Dear Jack,   Apr. 20, 1942

Did you hear about the Stanley Cup playoffs? Judge Morley and I listened to every game, alternating between his house and mine. We were jumping out of our seats at times. Game 4 in particular was a real nail biter and game 7 as well. I enclosed a summary of games 4–7. I'm sure as you read it you can imagine vividly the action.

I want to draw your attention to Frank Calder, the NHL president. As he is also of Scottish descent, it's quite possible that he is a distant relative. We have good genes, we Calder stock! I totally approve of his starting a tradition of giving a trophy to the most promising rookie of the year. Did you meet him during your time as sports editor for CP?

I don't know whether the national plebiscite on conscription draws as much attention as hockey. Perhaps they are held equally in the public regard. Of course, I continue my fascination with politics. The plebiscite was held and now Mr. King has to make up his mind whether to push legislation through to enforce conscription. The result was:

> 8 provinces recorded large majorities of "Yes" votes; Quebec alone voted "No" in heavy numbers and its attitude has the effect of depriving the country of that unanimous and overwhelming affirmative that was hoped for.
>
> Nevertheless, Canada has manifested to the world where it stands in this struggle. This further evidence of its faith in the common cause of freedom will reassure all of the United Nations that this Dominion stands staunchly with them and is eager to play its full part. In a word, the Canadian people pledge their all for victory in this crisis. (*Hamilton Spectator* editorial)

Obviously Mr. King is not going to want to alienate Quebec, so we'll have to wait and see what he decides. The matter might be dead in the water but the fact that English Canada voted so strongly to support the idea tells the world where we stand overall.

In other news, here in Canada, some POWs are enjoying the same type of freedoms as you lads. Take a look at this article about the Espanola Camp 21 life. From your letters it sounds as though you might be receiving some love letters from Irish colleens. I wonder if any of them have been charged with endangering national security!

Mary and Marjorie call us on Sundays and they are both living life to the fullest. Marjorie works under the auspices of J.A. McNeil, the general manager, who is a well-known theatre buff. The environment at CP is lively and challenging for her.

In spite of my disapproval of Mary's leaving home, I have to say she is doing very well in nursing. She loves the work and is full of enthusiasm when she phones.

We hear from Jake and Philip occasionally, only very short post cards or telegrams. Write as often as you can, dear boy. We live for the mailman's delivery. Your mother runs to the door and scans the bundle quickly for letters rather than bills. Much love, *Dad*

> April 18 — Toronto Maple Leafs win their Fourth Stanley Cup by defeating the Detroit Red Wings 4 games to 3 after being down to the Red Wings 3–0. The deciding Game 7 was played at Maple Leaf Gardens in Toronto.
>
> Commencing with the 1932–33 season, Calder named the top rookie in the NHL. Starting in 1936–37, he convinced the NHL's Board of Governors to let him buy a trophy to give annually to the league's top rookie, and he did this until 1941–42.[ii]
>
> The Espanola (Camp 21) POWs have enjoyed an active camp life with a theatrical group and soccer teams, but, they have also been put to work outside the camp in the area lumber industry. As lumber men they engage in the social activities in logging camps such as dances.
>
> They are very popular with the local ladies. "They are a fine class of people, we think. The girls are crazy about them and they have a pretty good time. As far as wanting to escape, you couldn't drive them away."
>
> Fraternizing with these popular enemy aliens came to a head when charges were laid against five teenage girls in Espanola under the Defence of Canada Regulations.

Five smitten local girls had been writing love letters to the POWs and among the gifts they'd sent were forbidden items such as cameras. On March 23, 1942, five Espanola teens pleaded guilty to the charges and were given suspended sentences. (Source: Ontario Regiment RCAC Museum, Espanola, Ontario).

Dear Jack, April 30, 1942

How are you? I hope you are well even though in prison. Mother and Dad think it's safer than being in a bomber over Germany.

I must confess that whenever I am nursing a young male patient, I am imagining it is you. I've had one guy for the past week who is really cute; he had to have an arm amputated after a farming accident. Only 19 years old, he lost his arm in a threshing machine. Florence Nightingale calls nursing "God's business." We tend not only the body but the soul. This boy is brave but he really needs someone to talk to. He often babbles like a child who is lonely and scared. The other day he asked me, "Do you think I'll ever have a girlfriend?" Of course I reassured him and told him how handsome he is.

My dorm room is near the chapel and on Friday evenings I hear the voices singing vespers, ghostly and gorgeous. The beautiful harmonies wafting down the hall create peace that's lovely as I'm falling asleep. I am trying to write a poem about it, but it's difficult to find time alone when I can concentrate.

I am rooming with the most wonderful girls. Dottie is American, from Michigan. She's my best friend. Also there's Linda and Sue in our room and the four of us always find something fun to do together. Occasionally if we're all off duty we take the bus and go to a movie. The nuns are quite strict about curfew so we absolutely have to be back on time.

Sometimes we go for a walk in the nature sanctuary near St. Peter's Seminary. If we're lucky we run into a couple of young priests. Why is it that the handsomest guys go in for a life of celibacy? We flirt like crazy with them but no bites so far. I wonder what would happen if one of them kissed one of us? Would he be expelled?

Other times we walk around the campus. I know you loved your life at U of T but you had nowhere to walk except downtown Toronto; Western has a more beautiful campus. Them's fighting words, eh. Well, I know a thing or two. Besides, I'm a grown woman now and I've studied anatomy and biology; I could probably teach you something — out behind the garden shed, that is!

Remember when we were teenagers and Marjorie and I discovered you boys smoking behind the garden shed in Goderich? And we threatened to tell Dad if you didn't let us try too? And I nearly choked? Are you still smoking? In case you don't know, it's very bad for your health. Try to limit yourself to just a few each day; that's what I do.

My favourite author, L.M. Montgomery, just died. I read all the Anne books, plus *Rilla of Ingleside*. I even had first editions on my bedroom shelf. I received them as birthday gifts, remember? She really understood the mind of a girl, what she thinks about, what she dreams of, what drives her. In her obituary I read that she herself had a very sad life that inspired her to write about a spunky character like Anne who overcame every difficulty.

Jack, I think about you every day, wondering what you are doing to pass the time in prison. How many of you are on the Allied side of the Curragh? Have you met any nice Irish girls? Do you still dream of flying? Being suspended in the sky at night would be amazing. Jack, I get why you want to fight the enemy, drop bombs even, considering what they have done. I just hope that when you come home you won't be changed from the sweet, funny brother I know. Stay safe and come home in one piece. Love, *Mary xoxo*

Dear Ann,   May 4, 1942

I'm enjoying the time we've spent together since New Year's Eve with our group of eight, but I want to get to know you better. We don't have time without the crowd, so would you write to me and fill me in on some personal details?

I bet you were a horse loving girl. What else did you like to do? Who are your closest friends, other than the ones I've met, and why do you like being with them? Do you have a favourite place? What do you think of Ireland? What makes it different from UK? Do you miss home when you're over there?

I know you have a great sense of humour because you are always kidding around, teasing me, and you have a very keen wit. No matter what I say you have a comeback. I hope you are not trying to put me off because you have the opposite effect on me.

I met your father at the pub and he invited me for a drink. I like him and enjoy talking to him on all sorts of topics. He likes his Guinness and horses and winning at the track. I thought we got along quite easily even though we have little in common. Do you think he invited me for a drink because he'd learned that we are seeing each other socially? I have not yet met your mother but I bet she's a lot like you, beautiful, intelligent, a bit shy, a bit funny, and quite capable. I suppose your father buys and sells the horses, runs the stables, grooms, and jockeys while your mother organizes the social life, the household, and gardens.

I don't mind telling you that one of my favourite places was the screened-in porch of our home. Some members of my family could always be found there during a thunder storm. We would sit in the dark listening to the rumble and crash of the thunder, then count the seconds until the lightning flashed. The number of seconds told us how far away the storm was, so we thought. I don't know if this is supported by any scientific evidence.

My research on Irish history is keeping me busy and I have a number of interviews to conduct. Each one leads me to another and another and another. It's a bit like falling down Alice's rabbit hole. I'm not sure when to stop research and start writing. It's a very seductive topic.

Speaking of 'seductive,' you have quite a way about you, a way that I find intriguing. I am writing because I miss you and wish we could see more of each other. I'm surprised you don't have a steady boyfriend. Is there someone I don't know about? Maybe some guy in the UK?

If you're not committed, would you please have dinner with me, just the two of us?

Yours, *Jack*

Dear Jack, May 15, 1942

Your mother and I are fine and grateful that spring is in full flush. The daffodils and tulips are poking up in the garden, and other green shoots, whose names I do not know, look promising. I hope you are enjoying similar spring notes in Ireland. Judge Morley and I walked nine holes of the golf course the other day. Our feet were quite damp when we arrived home, but it was great to see the greens and smell the muddy air. We can return with our clubs May 24th weekend. Have you had a game yet this year?

I've been following with interest the stories of POW camps in Canada in hopes that you might find inspiration in some of these escape attempts. All it takes is one idea that works, so keep trying. I've enclosed another clipping for you to share with the boys. Again I emphasize that securing safe houses will be essential to your success.

The following questions continue to circle the chambers of politicians and pundits: are there enemies among us who help POWs escape? Can one admire the ingenuity of escape when the attempt is made by the enemy? Are many of the POWs, in fact, sympathetic individuals? I have no doubt, were you here, that your pen would have fun with these mysteries.

Jake writes to us fairly regularly. He mentions that he plans to visit you at the end of the month. I hope the two of you will go out on the town.

I'm afraid I must write a homily and a sermon for tomorrow. God bless you, my dear son, and keep you safe. All my love, *Dad*

THE ONES THAT GOT AWAY

Although quite a few of the Canadian POW escapees got far, only two got away — a great record for Canada.

Luftwaffe pilot Walter Manhard, a Gravenhurst POW managed to trick the Veteran Guard into believing he had drowned while swimming. Sightings have been reported as far away as upper New York state.

The other more famous escapee, who had tried to escape several times in Britain after his capture as a downed pilot in September 1940, was Oberleutnant Franz von Werra.

Less successful but noteworthy escape attempts involved dummies and a Canadian U-boat sting operation. The dummy incident involved Leutnant Erich Boehle who escaped with Oberleutnant Peter Krug from Camp 30 at Bowmanville with the collusion of Bowmanville's POW complement. Krug and Boehle, dressed as workmen and guarded by a POW dressed in a Canadian Army Uniform (thanks to the camp's theatrical troupe) made their escape over two fences they were purportedly repairing while their POW cohorts as a distraction wildly cheered on a soccer game. Supplied with maps, currency and forged documents smuggled into Camp 30, the pair made it to Union Station in Toronto.

Boehle headed towards the USA via Niagara. When the Niagara Police Department phoned Camp 30 to ask them to check out Boehle's absence, they were told no one was missing. Two roll calls later, Commandant Lieutenant Colonel Roland O. Bull M.C. of Camp 30 still insisted that there were no missing POWs. Finally, when an oral count took place, Boehle's and Krug's escapes became evident.

The enterprising theatrical group had manufactured two very convincing dummies using papier-mâché, uniforms and paper stuffing. During the roll calls, ersatz officers Boehle and Krug were held in position by POWs on either side. Krug, who crossed at Windsor in a rowboat with oars he hastily cobbled together, was captured in San Antonio, Texas. He had made it that far due to safe house contacts he had from the German Abwehr/Spy Agency. In his hotel room the FBI found a .32 calibre handgun purchased from a pawn shop.

The U-boat sting operation involved U-boat commander Kapitaenleutnant Wolfgang Heyda. German Admiral Doenitz had planned Operation Kiebitz to spring several high profile naval officers including his own former adjutant and Otto Kretschmer, a U-boat ace called the Atlantic Wolf. The men were going to tunnel out and make their way to Chaleur Bay where U 536 would scoop them off Canadian shores.

When the tunnelling part of Operation Kiebitz fell through, Heyda decided to take advantage of the rendezvous point with his own daring plan. With civilian clothing, false papers, a rope boatswain's chair and nails hammered into his boots to make them into crampons, Heyda hid out in a shed until he could scale a fence pole and then attach himself to wires going over the fence using the boatswain's chair. Protected from electrocution by the rope of the chair, Heyda slid to freedom. A dummy stood in for him at roll call.

Canadian authorities, however, knew of Heyda's escape attempt and let him make it as far as Pointe de Maisonette. They used Heyda and a signal light to lure waiting U 536 into the sting. German U-boat Commander Schauenberg, suspicious of noises on his hydrophones did not surface for the pick-up. He evaded the depth charges of the Canadian destroyers and found his way out to the Atlantic.

U 536 survived, but not for long. The Royal Canadian Navy sunk it six weeks later. Heyda was returned to Camp 30.

Another pair of escapees gave up after trying to cross over the Arctic to get from Canada to Germany.

Twenty-eight of 80 hopeful escapees made it out of the Angler POW camp in Alberta with almost all of them captured quickly but for a pair who made it to Medicine Hat before they were picked up and returned.

Dear Mom, May 15, 1942

I'm feeling rather discouraged. A famous reporter from the *New Yorker* magazine is visiting the camp interviewing everyone who will sit down with him. He's even been caught eavesdropping in the bar. I'm afraid he's scooping my ideas for a series of articles, and there's nothing I can do about it. Some of the lads are eager to see their names in print. Even though they would consider themselves friends of mine, they don't realize how journalism is competitive and this is my story, not some interloper's. They don't mean to be disloyal. The NCOs are just young and ignorant of how their mouthing off will shut down my chances of being the first Canadian to report on the Curragh and Irish sensibility. I'm worried because, to be honest, Sam Boal is a damn fine writer who is sure to steal my thunder (Keefer, 221–231). I've been hiding out in my room avoiding contact with him. Anyway, if you happen to see a copy of the next *New Yorker*, would you pick one up for me please? I hate to admit it, but I'd like to see what he writes. Enough of my whining.

We prisoners are actually very fortunate to be tucked safely away in our little corner of Ireland. The huts are cleaned regularly by a crew of Irish women. It's funny that I can hardly understand them when they speak; either the accent is very thick or they speak Gaelic, in part or in whole. I'm sure they are as perplexed as I am; we stare at each other, shrug, smile, and go about our business.

We are hearing encouraging rumours that American troops are moving into Northern Ireland. This is positive news for several reasons. It means that Germany is less likely to invade Ireland; de Valera, the Prime Minister of Éire, will perhaps be persuaded to drop the neutrality position; and if that happens, we Allied prisoners will be freed. Now that America has entered the war we have more than its protection for convoys across the Atlantic. The United States can use Northern Ireland as a jumping off base for operations in Europe. I'm also hearing of aircraft refurbishing and repair factories being established. There's lots of employment for Irish folks.[iii] Both Belfast and Dublin were bombed a year ago,[iv] and they won't likely be again now that the Blitz is over, not with the American presence in the North.

I had an interesting letter from a fellow POW in Poland who came across a library established in the prison, and guess who heads up the selection of books? None other than C.S. Lewis, with J.R.R. Tolkien. Lewis sent out a broad appeal to all the major denominations for contributions of unmarked books and/or money for new books, and libraries in German prisons all over Europe are being established. What a fine idea. I have listened to a few of Lewis's broadcast lectures over BBC and found him to be a very articulate speaker.[v] Perhaps I can ask John Kearney to link the Curragh to Lewis's library programme. Maybe I'll even write to Lewis himself. I know he teaches at Oxford University.

Well, that's cheered me up considerably. Just having a chat with you, Mom, has done the trick to lift my mood. I love you so much. *Jack*

Dear Jack,   **May 24, 1942**

I was quite surprised to receive your letter. Thank you. Yes, I noticed that the group of us have sort of divided up into pairs. You've even held my hand a few times. No words were spoken, but our eyes did lock now and then. How do I feel about all this? Where shall I begin? I will tell you a bit about my youth.

As a girl I was only interested in horses. I rode my pony at age three; there are pictures! For my twelfth birthday I got my own horse and I was responsible for her: to feed her, muck out her stall, groom and exercise her. She was a chestnut mare Irish hunter, part thoroughbred, part Hanoverian. She came to me as a six-year-old named Molly-by-golly. She was a dream to ride. She loved to go cross county — jumped fences and hedges with ease. Of course, I wasn't allowed to go out alone with her at first, but when my parents saw how we had bonded, how she actually looked after me as much as I looked after her, they were impressed and gradually granted us more and more freedom. We were a great team and won ribbons frequently. There were always weekend events to look forward to. My dad was very involved in organizing so he was happy to trailer Molly. Most of the kids in the neighbouring counties were involved too; that was our social time.

Three of us usually won top ribbons. Dorothea O'Donnell was my main competitor and I hated her. She was such a cheater and would do anything to win. The other girl was Mary Kelly and she was my best friend so she hated Dorothea as well. The two of us used to plot how we could win instead of her, but we never cheated. So that's my code, you see. I can't stand a cheater.

As a teenager I was tall for my age and no boy would come near me. Besides, the only boys I knew were the same ones I had grown up with and they were more like cousins, if they weren't in fact cousins. They were totally immature. Mary and I considered those boys beneath us. We were saving ourselves for a real man, a handsome man of the world. We saw men like this at horse events, but they were too far above us; we were caught in the middle between childhood and adulthood, with no suitable dates.

You have the advantage over me in that you have met my father and have travelled a bit in the neighbourhood where I grew up. I have only your word that you are a poor preacher's kid, prone to getting into trouble with your brothers. You have good manners which I attribute to your mother. On the plus side you signed up to fight the Germans, a decision I deeply respect. (I am not one of those Irish who declare neutrality from every soap box.) The fact that you became a navigator speaks to your ability to discipline and train yourself to a difficult task requiring maths. This talent I admire as I also love maths.

I guess I would have to say that my favourite place is the stables. I spend hours there with Molly. I love to groom her. Brushing down the flanks of your horse is very meditative and relaxing and she loves it too. If I close my eyes I can smell her warm breath on my chest, feel her nuzzle me afterwards. We have a deep understanding of each other; she can read my moods and responds in kind.

I am an only child so I turn to my horse when you might turn to your brothers.

Well Jack, I thought this was going to be a short, courteous letter! I surprise myself by rambling. Yes, I'll have dinner with you. Meet me in Dublin on Sat. at 6 o'clock outside the library of Trinity College. From there we can walk to any number of pubs where you can regale me with stories about all the distress you caused your parents. Sincerely, *Ann Mitchell*

Dear Dad, Aug. 5, 1942

How are you and Mom faring? I've been working hard on my book about Irish history. You may notice a few excerpts smuggled out of the Curragh for publication. Don't know when CP will issue them.

I've been promoted to Flying Officer. Big deal, eh. I don't know how to think about that. Not much good being a FO if there's no opportunity to fly. On the other hand, maybe it's a hopeful sign that de V. plans to release us.

We heard from the diplomat, Sir John Maffey that there is talk of moving us twenty-five miles north of Dublin to another camp at Gormanston. Fleming heard rumours that the new camp would have no parole; and furthermore that new arrivals are not imprisoned; they are simply being escorted to the border. Maffey denied both of these. "Keep your spirits up, chaps. Stiff upper lip, and all that. The Irish will release you any day now; it's just a matter of time. I wouldn't advise any escape plans for the present. Keep quiet. That way you'll be released. At least, that's my hunch." He's not promising. We definitely can't count on him.

We tried negotiating with the IRA. After many meetings in Jammet's pub, one of the waitresses, named May — I've mentioned her before — a tall, striking redhead, slender with intense blue-green eyes, made friends with Fleming and eventually offered us a plan. The IRA, with half a dozen soldiers, would break into the Curragh at night in a large lorry, drive straight through the gate, smashing it to pieces, guns blazing if necessary, and rescue us for £500/ea. They would either bribe the road blocks or shoot their way through. Then we'd take the back roads north to the border. We worried that someone might be killed. We worried about the money. We talked day and night until we were blue in the face.

Finally, the day came that we had to pay or shut up. We met May at Jammet's and slipped her an envelope with £300, promising the rest when they showed up and broke us out for sure. She took the money and placed it under a certain plate at table four. It was raining hard that day. A man from Tipperary was expected to complete the deal. Before long, a tall, pale man entered the pub, wearing an old trench coat, boots, and rumpled tweed pants. He hung his hat and coat by the door, made eye contact with May, and walked immediately to table four. He was unshaven and wore a navy blue flannel shirt that covered a large stomach. "Sure this guy is going to save us," whispered Bobby. The man quickly pocketed the envelope of bills. Bobby leaned towards me again. "Bet we never see the great rescue truck." And he was right. So ended our adventure with the IRA.

Tell Mother that I'll write to her very soon. I promise her an even more exciting letter, I hope. Love to all, *Jack*

Dear Mom, Aug. 30, 1942

Bobby and Fleming (our commanding officer) have escaped. I'm happy for them, but bummed out that myself and the others are still here. By the way, I hope you and Dad are doing well. Thanks for your letters of encouragement. News from home is always welcome. Here's the great escape story:

Bobby and his brother Eddy used to spend summers working on the Erie Canal. Recently he remembered a farm gate that the two of them used to swing on and he put that memory together with a gate into the prison yard. It is located behind the guards' firing range so we never go to that particular corner, but we have seen trucks entering the compound bringing supplies by a road through that gate. Bobby wondered if the farm gate and the gate into the prison were the same construction.

Four of us decided to suss it out, so we crawled on our bellies (below the shots being fired by the guards!) from the golf course through the gorse to a point where we could see that the gates are attached by a simple L bracket. All we would have to do is lift the gates off the L and they would fall open. Only problem, the gates are each 6' wide and 12' high, hence very heavy.

Not to be deterred, we rescued a pair of curtain rods from the NCOs' shower hut and stowed them in the bicycle shed. They could support the gates as they were being lifted and spread the weight.

The weekend of the Irish Derby everybody who is anybody gathered at the racetrack. We took parole and mingled with the crowd, searching for contacts who might provide safe houses. Bobby talked to Aubrey Brabazon, one of the famous jockeys of Kildare, also head trainer at the Aga Khan stud farm, who had offered to put him up in one of the stables. Bobby cornered him and asked for specific directions.

The Aga Khan stud farm has three or four tracks and several hundred stables. "Go to the row of stables at the back of the estate. Inside the last one along the back wall at the right, you will find a ladder leading up to a small landing with a trap door. Climb through that to a low loft. You'll have to stay lying down and be absolutely quiet during the day when the grooms and stable boys are working. You can come out at night to stretch. Good luck, lads."

Bobby also asked Major O'Sullivan, our Christmas dinner host, if he was still willing to help. He said, "If you ever do get out, you can count on me. I'm not about to break any laws, but ... enough said."

We had decided not to let the others know in case word slipped out to warn the guards, as possibly happened last time. The night of Aug. 17 was moonless; we called a meeting, announced the plan and asked for volunteers. Everyone was in. Four of the strongest guys agreed to lift the gates off the L brackets. My job, with Wolfe, was to overpower the guard at the parole hut and jam a bicycle into the open gate (Keefer, 203). The internees would slip through into the alley between the two barbed wire walls. Covington was appointed to jam a corkscrew into the lock of the police hut so that they would be blocked.

We all dressed in dark clothing, blacked our faces, and strapped our escape packs to our backs. Some wore strips of mattress around their arms and legs to protect them from the barbed wire. Everything went according to plan. Just when the four strongest were on the verge of lifting the gate, a guard peered through the darkness directly at Bobby and raised his gun. The boys froze. The guard crept closer in the pitch black. Suddenly Bobby yelled, 'Go!" The gate rose and fell towards the guard, knocking the gun from his hand. As many men as possible scrambled through the opening and over a 5' wire barrier. I was last, so Sgt. Kelly got me and gave me a good whack with his club, but he didn't get my head.

Nine men got out. Most of them were recaptured within 24 hrs., but Girdlestone, the New Zealander, hid for five days with an Irish family. They were driving him north when a high-speed chase ensued, ending with his arrest and return to the Curragh.

Bobby and Fleming are still on the lam. I expect by now they have walked at night to Northern Ireland and are back in the fold of the RAF flying ops and having the time of their lives. Mom, I miss them, and naturally my hut seems empty now without Bobby. Parole is cancelled again and more wire has been erected around the compound (Keefer, 188–201).

I'll figure something out. Love to all, *Jack*

My Darling, Sep. 26, 1942

I find myself thinking of you all the time. With Bobby and Fleming gone, with increased wire fencing around the compound, with my series on Irish neutrality and the Curragh scooped by that interloper Sam Boal from the *New Yorker*, all my motivation is gone for sensible things like writing and escape plans. I wallow in a labyrinth of thoughts that ultimately go nowhere. My purpose in signing up to fight the enemy is thwarted. What am I doing here? My only answer is that the gods have smiled on me and brought me in touch with you, my lovely Ann.

This summer we've enjoyed many private times together. Walks down country lanes, dinners in pubs, dancing in the moonlight on the lawn of your parents' estate — no matter what we do our time is memorable. Even when you're teaching me to ride, we laugh and have fun. The horses seem to know that love is in the air when they nuzzle us as we're brushing them.

Since the day of our picnic, when we swam in the pond, that deep cool water, secluded, private, when the whole world faded away and we existed only for each other, I realized I have loved you for months. Now all I can think of is you, my sweetheart. How could I have been so slow? You light up the room for me and I want to see more of you.

Do you know, I told my mother that I would not fall for any particular girl during the war because that wouldn't be fair. Now I've changed my mind. I want to enjoy everything life has to offer. I want to love you to the roots of my being.

That image of us in the pool, my arms wrapped tightly around your body, your skin so silky, your hair shining auburn in the afternoon sun, your kisses on my lips, all my senses sing and I want you again and again. Your face fills my days, your dark Irish eyes, your perfect nose, your enigmatic smile, my very own Mona Lisa. I imagine running my fingers all over your face, through your hair, down over your breasts; like a blind man I am discovering you, inch by inch. You are my delight.

Shall I continue? Are you convinced? I, Jack Calder, have fallen in love with Ann Mitchell of Rathbone Lane, Ballynure, Co. Wicklow, Ireland, Earth, Universe. I swear it on the bones of my ancestors. I swear it on the blood of our unborn children. This is my sacred vow. Yours, *Jack*

Dear Jack, Oct. 1, 1942

Well! You don't waste time. We've known each other for only nine months.

I wasn't going to say anything, but I think we rushed, that day in the pool. Don't get me wrong — the whole experience had an impact on me and I do like you, Jack. As a woman, perhaps, I am more vigilant than you. We must take precautions; otherwise we might have a little surprise.

I am not averse to having children, when the time is right; however, I'd like to avoid pregnancy until the war is over.

Which brings me to my next reason for hesitancy: will you go home to Canada when you are discharged? I'm not trying to trap you, Jack; you can be frank with me. We can continue dating until you go home if that is your wish. I don't want to stop seeing you.

I might be falling for you. You're handsome, in an Irish sort of way with your hazel eyes, red hair and freckles. You're also very charming, and fearless, characteristics I like. I'd go so far as to say you have a good chance. Let's see how we go over the next few months.

I'm thrilled that you think so much of me. I enjoy being with you, Jack. You are very tender when you touch me, not pushy or aggressive like some bully-boys. I like to run my fingers through your hair or down your neck to your lovely back. A girl can feel the muscles in your shoulders even through your sweater, and without your clothes, well, that's one of my favourite memories. Our swim in the pool wasn't really swimming, was it. I'm surprised we didn't drown, but you were strong enough to keep us both afloat.

Tell me about your sister, Mary, and your other sister, Marjorie, who works for CP, same as you did. Are you close? I wish I had siblings. I have dozens of cousins, but that's not the same relationship. I can't understand how parents divide their love and attention when they have six or more children as lots of Irish families do. I remember the priest preaching about the blessings of large families and looking down from the pulpit directly at my father. It was embarrassing. I'd like you to tell me more about growing up in a large family. Do you think it influenced your character? People say only children are inclined to be selfish and entitled. I hope I am not; my parents would be mighty disappointed.

My thoughts are also racing around that labyrinth you mentioned. I'm not sitting on the fence to tease you. I just don't know for sure if my current feelings are good for the long haul. I don't know if I should be holding back, preparing myself for

the inevitable time that we will say good-bye when you go back to Canada. I run between the many sweet memories I have of being with you to the many problems of a long-distance relationship. Can you be patient while I mull over my thoughts?
Ann

Hey Jack,   **Oct. 8, 1942**

I'm in Canada. The dream of writing our own ticket and getting back to flying ops did not happen. I was ordered to take 2 weeks leave and then report to Dorval as an instructor (Keefer, 71). What a come down.

I suppose you're anxious to hear about the rest of our escape. We ran south first, and then doubled back towards the Aga Khan estate. We found the last of many stables, discovered the ladder and the little door into the loft. The space was all of 3' high, so we could only crawl or lie down. We waited four days, passing the time with word games and math challenges. Our meals were turnip and small bites of sausage. Ugh. At night we climbed down the ladder for drinks of water and a splash in the horse trough. Needs must, eh. Four days passed, and then five days. We realized that Col. O'Sullivan wasn't going to show, so we started walking. Fleming had a map.

We stayed off the main roads. Loping along the side roads in the dark was pleasant after being holed up. If someone came, we dodged into a hedge until they passed.

Surprise, surprise, Fleming had arranged with his girlfriend to hide us. That's a war hero for you — always has Plan B up his sleeve. I was a bit miffed that he hadn't told me during our five days in the attic, but I kept my mouth shut. It wasn't the first time that Fleming had held his cards to his chest. At dawn of the sixth day we arrived at Kelly's estate in Salina, north of Naas. Fleming threw a few pebbles at Mary's window. She woke up and whispered, "Go to the barn!" Eventually she and her parents brought hot food, tea and cookies. Boy was that ever good.

Mr. Kelly informed us that only three internees were still at large. Rumour had it that the third was Sgt. Newport and he was already in the North. Apparently Girdlestone was nabbed in a biscuit factory in Dublin after the Garda chased him there in the company of two members of the notorious Escape Club. Trust Gird to put his hat in with that lot. No wonder he got caught.

That afternoon Mr. K told us that all the soldiers at the roadblocks and in the fields with dogs had packed up and left. The next morning, disguised as cattle drovers, we cycled with Mr. K north to Kilcock where we were introduced to Major Aylmer who lived in Courtown. His house — oh my god, Jack — was the grandest of any we saw our whole time in Ireland.

The final link in the chain was a retired Royal Navy officer known only as the Captain. He lived north in Monaghan on a cattle farm. We arrived about 3 a.m. and met a large, friendly, bearded old sailor who poured us each several stiff glasses of — what else — Irish whiskey! He thought our drover costumes were a laugh and convinced us to act like his Australian cousins. We brushed up our accents to work in the field the next day pitching hay with his farm hands. You know what, Jack? It came upon me in that field how resentful I feel towards Ireland. In spite of the great golf games with you, all the capers we had, dates with girls, talks late at night, I wish I'd never laid eyes on the place.

The Captain led us to the border just south of Roslea. We followed a path two miles through the woods until we reached a red mailbox with a distinctive coat of arms. Then we went looking for the Royal Ulster Constabulary building. After we banged on the door it opened to reveal three policemen with guns. We ID'd ourselves, showed our dog tags, and were admitted and given one phone call. I reached the C.O. at RAF base, Aldergrove. An hour later an RAF Wingco drove up in a Jaguar convertible with the top down. Boy, were we glad to see him. He drove us to Belfast. We were billeted for a day with a retired army officer where we slept around the clock. The next morning we flew to London in a four-seater German Fokker.

Anyway, Jack, that's the whole story. You can dress it up if you like. I bet you're working on Plan C, D, or F to break out of there. Contact me when you do and we'll get together. I'm anxious to know how you've been. Good luck, buddy. *Bobby K* (Keefer, 246–48)

My Darling Ann, Oct. 10, 1942

You didn't respond to my declaration! I understand your reluctance. I love you with every fibre of my being. You will break my heart if you turn me down.

You say the passion of the moment swept you off your feet. You say the blue uniform was your father's dream for you to marry, and yet when we two swam in that pool, remember, there was no blue uniform. That was such an honest moment. Tell me if it's not true. I trust you were following your heart when you kissed me and came to me so eagerly.

You have brought up the question of where we would live after the war. What about England as a compromise? My family would be disappointed for sure, but travel will open up for everyone after the war. I want them to come here and see all that I have seen. I want to take you to Canada, and show you the special places of my youth, introduce you to many people who are important to me.

Oh Ann, my dear, these worries can be overcome. Think of all the couples we know who have made the leap into an international marriage. Five couples from the Curragh alone have taken vows. And I am not one to jump on the band wagon. That's not my style. You know me well enough to believe that I am a man who makes up his own mind.

I did not suddenly wake up one day and want to fall for the first colleen who came along. You are a very special girl, a unique treasure. I am just grateful that I beat all those other fellows who wanted to dance with you on NY Eve. Remember how we fit perfectly in each other's arms as we swirled around the room? I could just as easily say that I fell in love with your blue gown, as you say that you fell for my blue uniform. But we know there's more to it than that, don't we, my dear?

I am sure that your heart will lead you to the right answer. 'Loving you is as natural as breathing.' Whoever said that knows how I feel. We found each other, my darling. Be glad. Yours, *Jack*

Dear Jack,   **Dec. 31, 1942**

How are you, my dear boy? Your father and I are doing fine as far as our health goes, but we're feeling saddened by a terrible tragedy here in Canada. In fact, it happened not too far from here in Almonte, just a few days ago, Dec. 27th. A troop train slammed into the back of one carrying passengers resulting in 36 deaths and injuries to over 100 persons. While none of the soldiers on the troop train were injured, several servicemen on the passenger train were killed including two cousins from Chalk River, 28-year-old Private Eldon MacDonald and 22-year-old Trooper Charles MacDonald. (I don't know if you know them or have even heard of them, but some of your friends might have.)

Your father grabbed the first bus he could and travelled to Almonte to help console the families. The community really came together. Stories are emerging of the heroes who responded to the tragedy, such as the doctors and nurses from neighbouring towns who answered the call for help and the many Almonte residents who opened up their homes to the injured.

Sadly, John Howard, the conductor of the troop train, took his own life. He was only a few months away from retirement but as the most senior crew member on the troop train, Howard carried a heavy burden, devastated by how many lives had been lost in the crash. He left a note for his family explaining he could not live with the blame for deaths of all of those people. His body was found in the Rideau River, near his home in Smiths Falls. Your father visited his widow and children who are suffering terribly as they lost not only their husband/father but many friends as well.

Apparently the crash happened at a very dangerous curve just at the entrance to Almonte. Blame is being spread all around. As I understand, most accuse the crew of the troop train for not staying twenty minutes behind the passenger train, travelling too fast and not being prepared to stop when entering Almonte. However, the passenger crew is sharing responsibility for not using a flare at the Almonte station to warn the other train that they had been losing time during their entire journey.

The Theatre, located just a few metres from the crash site, was used as a first aid centre. The Old Town Hall housed the dead. The Rosamund Hospital treated the most seriously injured patients in the immediate minutes after the accident. Almonte has never experienced such a night. An inquest has been called in hopes to prevent recurrence of such a catastrophe.

Your father and I are counting our blessings that you boys are safe. Such events bring our families closer to our hearts. Why are some unlucky and die young while others enjoy a full lifetime? Such mysteries obsess me at times like these. I pray daily for you boys and at the same time wonder why God would favour us. Your father admonishes me to have faith, but that's his job. I wonder what he thinks really, in his heart of hearts. He seldom shares any doubts. We lost Gerald in a senseless act that has shaken me to the core and still affects my faith. Now I pray blindly but don't expect God to answer.

How is your faith, my boy, you who have suffered the horrors of war? Do you have peace of mind? You turned twenty-seven this past year, you're a man, but I'm still your mother. When you children were all home, we used to debate these mysteries around the dinner table, remember?

It's time for bed. I do wish you a very Happy New Year, Jack. Write soon and share some good news from Ireland. Love, *Mom xo*

Part Three

1943

Darling Ann,   Jan. 10, 1943

I owe a huge thank you to you and your family for a wonderful Christmas. All of you could not have shown this homesick lad a nicer time. Our traditions are so alike that I felt quite natural in your midst. Sadly, missing were my dear parents, my brothers (having Christmas alone god knows where), and my sisters at home. But your folks were great and wonderful fun, so a light-hearted time was had by all in spite of the war.

    We did manage to have our own little bit of paradise and peace on Earth, didn't we, dearest. I won't forget those private moments that we shared. Your tender touches I will hold close to my heart. When I'm alone in my little hut in the Curragh (are you weeping for me yet?) I will have beautiful memories of the splendid colours of the house decorated to the hilt, the magnificent dinner with all its fixings, the jokes and laughter, the songs around the grand piano, and again those few secluded moments we shared. I am such a lucky fellow.

    When the whole family gathered together for a cross-country ride, I tumbled into a storybook. My riding capabilities are questionable, as your father pointed out (!). My backside felt a bit bruised for a few days but I'm sure with practice I can toughen up. You ride elegantly, my dear, so graceful in the saddle. That poor nag I was bouncing on top of will likely run the other way the next time she sees me coming.

Seriously, Ann, I had a wonderful Christmas, thanks to you. I'll have to think of some appropriate way to show my appreciation to your parents.

As for New Year's Eve, you looked stunning in your red gown. Every eye was upon you when we took to the dance floor. You remind me of Scarlet O'Hara in *Gone with the Wind*. I could sense the power of that crimson to attract attention as we waltzed; every woman wanted to be you and every man wanted to be me. Shall we ever forget that night as long as we live? You, my darling, were the star of the evening.

As wonderful as the holiday was, I must discipline myself for the next few months and get down to some serious writing on my book. I learned so many crazy anecdotes from your cousins, aunts and uncles that I must write down before I forget; those funny stories of peculiar Irish ways are just the juice I need to add colour to the dry bits of history. I want to do justice to the book and that is going to take dedication on my part. I'm afraid you're a major distraction for me, dearest. It takes me quite a while to recover my senses and get down to work when I return to my typewriter.

I think of you every day, always with a happy heart. At last I have a photograph of you! Thank you, my darling. How beautiful you are. I could gaze at your face for hours. You have given me joy in the midst of prison. What a complex journey this year is.

I long to be with you all the days and nights of my life. You are the air I breathe.

Yours forever, *Jack*

Dear Jack,   Feb. 11, 1943

Valentine's Day is just around the corner. You are the dearest, cleverest, most captivating man I ever met in my life. You are battering the ramparts of my heart. I think about our times together and try to recollect every word, every touch. Do you recall our walk down the lane last Saturday? Even holding hands and kidding around with you is a perfect memory. I keep replaying these treasures in hopes that they will not fade with time. I love the sound of your voice, especially when you sing me those corny Canadian folk songs. You make me laugh and forget our problems.

I wish that your parents and sisters could come across the pond for a visit with my family; and of course, your brothers would be back in England from wherever they are serving and they could come too. Your family would meet my family and we would all be so happy together. Many drinks would be shared in celebration. Maybe we would all go riding.

I wish you were free to stay with me for a weekend, dear Jack. I wish the war were over. I wish we lived in a cabin by the sea and had nothing to do but stare into each other's eyes, tell stories, and swim in the sea as the sun sets. You would have a desk overlooking the beach and would be working on a new book, maybe a novel. I would come into your private space and tease you with my fingers until you turned to me with an embrace so tender I'd lose my breath and urge you to follow me.

Are these pipe dreams, Jack? I know, but it's Valentine's Day. I'm usually a practical, no-nonsense girl, but you have changed me. Now I dare to dream.

I can't wait to see you again. I want to run into your arms and lean against you. I promise I will kiss you until you beg me to stop!

I will lock these memories as the happiest days of my life. Yours, *Ann*

Dear Jack,   Feb. 28, 1943

I have returned to England, assuming my post with WAFF. The work we are engaged in is exciting and should help the overall war effort. I wish I could share it with you but that will have to wait.

You'll never guess what happened on the ferry ride. It was a clear sunny morning, so there was no mistaking what we witnessed. The waves were gently rolling, almost calm by Irish Sea standards. We were pulling out of the harbour when all of a sudden the sea exploded in a huge geyser; I mean, a jet erupted hundreds of feet into the air, and a low boom rumbled across the ocean floor toward us. We rushed to the railing of the ferry as the sea surged and giant swells rolled their way across the surface of the sparkling water. The telltale smell of cordite burned in our nostrils. We gaped at each other and then began surmising about what had happened.

We concluded that a U-boat had run over a mine and immediately exploded. Then the wreckage began emerging from the deep, popping up one piece of flotsam at a time. I won't describe all the fragments and scraps in the debris field, but everything from the tragedy below — human limbs even, an officer's hat — emerged as we watched the surface of the sea being littered. A dreadful quiet descended upon us. Pretty soon Navy Defence appeared and the crew gathered chunks and remnants of the U-boat, hauling them onboard to be identified. What a sobering start to my day.

I can't help but think of the young men who lost their lives this morning. They wouldn't have known what hit them. I suppose they were as guilty as any German, but they were probably just boys following orders. I read that one captain of a U-boat was just 24 years old. That's younger than you, Jack. I don't know whether his heart was filled with hate. It's quite likely that this captain had a sweetheart; he definitely had a mother and father, friends, possibly siblings, as did every man onboard. A whole community either died or was aggrieved in this very small incident of the wider war.

I hope you don't think my thoughts are treasonous, Jack, as you are, after all, a fighting man yourself. Do you ever come home from a mission shattered, with such thoughts keeping you awake? You will share honestly with me, won't you, Jack? I am exposing my vulnerability to you. I hope you will reciprocate and furthermore, that we will always confess our deepest, most personal thoughts.

Tonight just as dusk was falling I heard the roar of Merlin engines so I rushed outside along with my neighbours. The sky was filling with a gaggle of Wellingtons and Lancasters. On and on they came, rows and rows of them, dozens, and then hundreds; they came from every aerodrome in England, a seemingly never-ending parade of 4-engine bombers. They streamed southward and the mighty roar of their passing was heard by everyone, the whole town and beyond — factory workers returning from a shift, housewives in their gardens, children playing, Land Army girls in the fields, and off-duty WAAFs like myself. We all gazed upward in awe.[vi] The sound was deafening and when it finished, the quiet assaulted our ears too. A neighbour shouted, "Jerry's going to get it tonight!" and we all cheered. I couldn't help myself — the flight had been so impressive. Now I'm thinking of their deadly mission, knowing that before dawn many will be killed. Oh Jack, I wish you were here to hold me.

I love you so terribly much, my darling. I'll see you in March when I have leave. We'll go out on dates as if the world is far away and we are safe. Good night, sweet Jack. Yours, *Ann*

Dear Ann,   **March 5, 1943**

You astound me with your deep humanity, my darling. I have read and reread your letter many times. You feel compassion for the enemy and understand the plight of a sailor, isolated in a U-boat, caught up in a war that he, perhaps, did not choose, persuaded by the popular movement in Germany. Even if he is strong for the other side, you feel sad that he lost his life fighting for something he believed.

The sight of the exploding U-boat has brought the war up close and personal for you. You've been raised in neutral Éire and, even though you work in England, you don't see the enemy face-to-face. Have you forgotten the bombings of London, Coventry, all of Europe? The homes of many have been destroyed, and the lives of young and old have been lost. There's scarcely a household that hasn't been struck to the heart. Remember for a moment who started the aggression. Those young men on the U-boat were shouting "Heil Hitler!" at the last rally they attended. They swore allegiance to their mission.

I hate the war too, but the only way Hitler will stop is if we make him. We must stand up to him, with bombs, yes, and mines. I sympathize with the loss of life, though. We're living through a horrible time, it's true.

I sleep from exhaustion after a mission. If I feel any guilt I remember the tyranny and terror that threaten to strike us down. We cannot focus on the lives below us; we must concentrate mainly on the precision of our work and our own safety. We take pride in being part of a great battle which is slowly bringing us closer to victory over a foe sworn to enslave the world's people. I heard a perfect quote of G. K. Chesterton: "The true soldier fights not because he hates what is in front of him, but because he loves what is behind him." We live with this paradox in our hearts.

I'll tell you something I've never told anyone. One night during a mission, another Lancaster had been flying just a few hundred yards ahead and to starboard of us. Suddenly the Lanc disappeared! All that remained was a small cloud of black smoke and some odd bits and pieces spinning through the air.[vii] Those are the boys I feel sorry for. They never knew what hit them. Moreover, they did not start this conflict. They are responding to an evil that is perpetrated against them.

I am working hard on my history of Ireland. Every day I start fresh in the morning, take lunch in my room, and work solid all afternoon until tea time. I use the evenings for walks and talks. Finally I have lined up an interview with Dan Breen, former IRA Commandant of the Third Tipperary Brigade, now a Fianna Fáil politician. He has promised to sneak me into the gallery for a session of Irish Parliament, the Dahl. I hope to see de V. himself in person arguing whatever is up for debate that day. I can't interview him because he is surrounded by security but I can talk to a number of political journalists at The Palace Bar on Fleet Street afterward. (Do you know the famous watering hole for journalists and writers? I'd love to run into Bertie Smyllie, editor of the *Irish Times*, or Brinsley MacNamara, whose short stories I love.)

I hope Dan Breen doesn't invite me to Dublin at the same time as your visit. That would be a shame. I want to spend every minute with you.

I have submitted two articles on Irish neutrality to CP and I'm waiting to hear from Gillis Purcell whether or not he's going to publish them. I'm planning a series of five articles, segments of my manuscript, and if they work their way into Canadian dailies, that will give me more credibility as a journalist writing about Éire.

My dearest Ann, you best know now, I'm not noted for my humility, but I do love you with a humble heart. I don't know what I would do without you. I am so sorry that I cannot be there with you when you go through moments that must be terrifying and upsetting. We will both have to rely on our dreams of being together to help us endure the present difficulties. Whenever I am lonesome for you I close my eyes and imagine touching you, smelling your hair, tasting your lips, hearing your voice. I have a catalogue of favourite memories I like to rehearse. I live over the times we were together, the things we said and the many things we should have said. Maybe you do too? We'll see each other soon, darling. Forever yours, *Jack*

Dear Jack,   **26 April, 1943**

Well, I am officially 54 years young this week. Thank you, dear boy, for the telegram and fruit basket. What a surprise! However did you manage it? Such a lovely variety and very prettily arranged. Small jars of jams and even honey were included, treats which will be enjoyed for months. I really feel spoiled to be showered with such luxury.

I have discovered a new treat. There's a novel type of biscuit in the store now called a nacho. I serve it with a bowl of my fruit chili sauce. The idea is to dip a nacho into the chili sauce and then quickly pop it into one's mouth before it drips onto clothing or worse, the carpet. When I first served it during our break from playing bridge with Judge and Maureen Morley, we laughed our heads off trying not to spill. Now she serves it too, so I guess I started a trend. I'll send you a package of nachos with a jar for dipping and you boys can try your luck.

Our fashions sure have changed since the beginning of the war. For starters, of course there is no silk anywhere to be found. Women are redesigning any silk they already own. I understand that ladies in Britain occasionally get their hands on a downed parachute which has miles of silk. How fortunate! The quality would be far tougher than that in a scarf. Wouldn't it be illegal to repurpose a parachute? I hear the Brits are limited to a line of clothing called Utility. Deborah Kerr certainly made a splash last year modelling Utility in the Picture Post. Mind you, she'd look good in a potato sack.

Another trend I'm noticing is wide-legged pants on women. I don't understand that trend as we're supposed to be saving fabric. We see these pants everywhere now, even on the streets, which is mildly shocking. You won't see your mother wearing wide-legged pants, I can assure you. I like dresses. They're cool in summer, and always respectable. I've heard of "siren suits" that women can don over pyjamas when the air raid sirens call everyone to the shelters. Now that's a practical item. I feel for the families with many children to clothe. Church bazaars don't always supply the needed sizes, but we do our best to circulate garments.

The newspapers are proclaiming that Rommel, "the Desert Fox," has been beaten in North Africa. Everyone is high with exuberance from the victory at El Alamein. We discuss it as the turning point of the war at every social gathering. Our mouths are all a-twitter with opinions about Montgomery's strategy; you'd think we knew what we were talking about. Ladies at a church bazaar arguing about tank movements in the Egyptian desert make me want to laugh, but I restrain myself and thank heaven for good news.

Well, it's time for bed. Thank you again, dear boy, for being so thoughtful.

Love, *Mom xo*

Dear Jack, June 27, 1943

I've been wanting to talk to you about something for a few weeks now. As our relationship is serious, I feel I can bring this to the table. It is only fair that I tell you my thoughts now; otherwise, down the road, I might be accused of being a hypocrite: I feel that there are three of us in this relationship.

We've been seeing less of each other, and writing less also. I know it's been quite some time since you've heard from me, and no doubt you've been wondering why. This letter is the most difficult I've ever had to write and you must realize how much it pains me. I've always been honest with you, Jack, and I believe you deserve only the truth from me.

You are obsessed with writing your book and it impedes your ability to relate to me. I realize you are a writer first and foremost, but if you sincerely want to have love in your life, a special love, then you must adjust your bachelor stance and make room. It is not enough to meet occasionally for a passionate embrace to be followed by weeks of silence while you write.

I respect your talent enormously. I respect you as a person. You are the finest man I have ever known. You say you love me, and I believe you, but our current relationship is not healthy for building a family of our own in the future. You have no balance in your life at the moment, and prison (even with parole) is no excuse.

I have not been happy for some time and you don't even notice. I am 28 years old. I can't wait for you to grow up and take this relationship seriously. This is not a fling for me as it appears to be for you.

I've tried to get your attention before; now I'm stating plainly: drop the book. You're not even Irish, for god's sake. Who do you think you are to try and define us? It's a ludicrous assignment. No one is asking you to write our history. You are a guest, a visitor, a tourist in our country. Please respect your limitations. Your vision is skewed by your experience as a prisoner of the Curragh. Whenever we do meet, our conversation is absorbed with questions about Ireland. We have discussed every chapter of your book ad nauseum. I'm sick of it. There's more to life, Jack, than your silly book.

Don't think for a moment that I don't love you, Jack. I most sincerely do. You are everything I've ever dreamed of in a husband. Lately I fear that my dreams are just that, dreams, mist, air. You fooled me into believing that you were committed to developing a mature, dedicated love. You wooed me and won me, and now you seem to have lost interest, except for a brief roll in the hay every so often. I adore the passionate way you make love to me, Jack, truly I do, but sex is not enough to build a marriage, if that's even what you intend.

Why should I pledge my life to someone who only wants to talk about Irish politics? I'm leaving Ireland behind because I'm tired of all this. I've heard it, north, south, east and west, my whole life, discussed amongst my parents and their friends. I was hoping we would have more to talk about because you're Canadian and have a broader perspective.

Jack, if I could spare you this heart-ache, I would. If we break up, I will feel the pain intensely too, but I can see no other way at the moment. You deserve to be happy and you will find someone who is independent enough to give you the time and space in your life to write to your heart's content. That person, however, is not me. I tried and now I have to face the truth about myself. I am not who you need. I cannot stay in our relationship. I want to move on with my life.

If you continue with your book, I wish you fabulous success and hope you will achieve great acclaim, for you so richly deserve it. You have dedicated yourself to this cause with a drive that is admirable. Good luck to you always. You were my first true love and I shall never forget you. I am honoured that you chose me, even for a brief time. I'm sure you will become famous and have an exciting life. All the best, *Ann*

Rathbone Lane, July 3, 1943
Ballynure,
Co. Wicklow,
Ireland

Dear Mr. & Mrs. Calder,

I am writing to you as a friend of your son, Jack, and at his request. By this time you will know that he has escaped from the Curragh and is safe in England. I use the word 'escaped' advisedly because Jack is not permitted to speak of how he managed his getaway. He signed confidentiality papers with the RAF to maintain his silence, but he wants you to know a little of the ruse he created with the help of some of us who believe in him. This letter is confidential and must not fall into the hands of the press. I will do my best to share some of the details so your minds can be at rest regarding this mystery.

The planning began as long ago as last Christmas holiday season when Jack and I were invited to dinner at the home of the High Commissioner for Canada in Ireland, John Kearney. He thought it a disgrace that Jack and the others had been held so long in the Curragh while, recently, militant flyers who landed by mistake in Ireland were repatriated, no problem. He knew of another case, of a Polish pilot who has a medical condition and his release is pending examination by two doctors. If they consent to write letters, that Pole will probably be released. We racked our brains to think of some medical condition that could be argued in Jack's case, but could think of nothing, because he is very healthy.

Jack himself came up with the idea of an attempted suicide (Keefer, 230–32), but we discounted that as being too dangerous; however, on the advice of my family doctor, a safe plan was devised. Now we had to invent a plausible reason that such a character as Jack, who always sees the bright side, would want to kill himself. The build-up of depression would take months but Jack was prepared to be patient and let the evidence unfold slowly. It would be important to convince the whole camp that Jack was not fooling around and that his attempt was really suicidal.

My part in the ruse was to write love letters to Jack, a happy job to which I readily agreed. He wrote to me very tenderly and I answered; so began a correspondence that became quite heated, I blush to admit. According to plan, I finally broke up with him.

We took into our confidence Sub-Lieut. Bruce Girdlestone, Jack's closest friend in the Curragh after Bobby and Grant escaped. Bruce is from New Zealand, is always kidding around, and above all, can tell a joke with a straight face. His role would be to discover Jack's attempted suicide just in time to save him.

Jack's part was multi-faceted. First would be drinking to excess. He made sure that all the camp believed him to be a heavy drinker, taking more and more bottles from the bar, often pouring the contents down the drain. He could act the part of being intoxicated very credibly.

Also Jack created the fiction that he was writing a book on Irish history. He even had Colonel McNally convinced; he would bring books for Jack to read and they had long discussions together. Everyone in camp was sick of hearing about 'the book,' and so was I. On the night in question, Jack laid out a hundred pages of his writing on the bed, along with my break-up letter.

Then he swallowed a prescribed amount of tincture of iodine. But first he had taken the antidote, sodium thio-sulphate, on the advice of my doctor, so let me assure you, Jack was never in any actual danger. At the pre-appointed time, he was discovered. Girdlestone was alerted and sprang into action to supervise the immediate trip to hospital. Jack was repatriated the following day.

I visited him yesterday at Halston, the RAF hospital in England. He is smiling from ear to ear and sends you his love and apologies for keeping you in the dark the past few months. There was no way to inform you without alerting the censors so we simply had to play the long game.

Jack is hopeful that he will soon be back in the big show, as the airmen call it. He is impatient to join the boys in the action and help put a stop to this war. I have to honour him for that.

Well, this has turned into a long explanation but Jack wanted you to know the story behind the scene. He has pledged his word to maintain silence on the matter so you can be sure he will never write the truth for the newspapers. Sincerely, *Ann Mitchell* (Keefer, *Grounded in Eire*)

London, England July 9, 1943
Dear Mom and Dad,

I'm so happy to be able to write freely to you at long last. By now you will have received Ann's letter and know the plot to have me released from Ireland's grasp. What a journey that has been! When the war is over I'll have a great story to tell, but not now.

Ann is a great gal. She lives in England most of the time. Her expertise is radar and she has a fine mind for it. I intend to see as much of her as possible between our duty schedules. We'll try to meet up in London at Minsky's or the Brevet Club in Berkeley Square. I'm excited to see some of my old friends very soon. Although Bobby Keefer and Grant Fleming are still in Canada, they'll be over here later this summer.

How are you both? I truly regret keeping you in the dark regarding my plot to escape but I just couldn't risk the censors getting a hold of the information and ruining my last chance at freedom. I hope you weren't too worried when you didn't hear from me for a long time during my "depression." At least you knew that I was safe, far from the battle.

Have you heard from Phil and Jake? This letter is coming to you by private carrier pigeon (a friend is going on leave in Canada). I can say now that they're with the British 8th army moving into Italy. When they take Sicily, Mussolini will be disgraced and deposed, probably within days. Hurrah for the Allies! Montgomery is known to be an excellent strategist, so we can count on him to get the job done. After my release from hospital yesterday I dropped in to the London office of CP where I heard these rumours from very reliable sources.

Tomorrow I return to the job. First on the agenda is retraining. Mom and Dad, we are winning this war. There are amazing new techniques in navigation developed in the twenty months that I was out of action; techniques to accurately mark targets during night bombing; techniques to identify enemy planes from as far away as eighty miles; new strategies of flying hundreds of bombers in a gaggle to increase the safety of each one.

I'm convinced that we're ahead in the game. You may have heard the news that four of Germany's top night fighter aces have been shot down.

I haven't seen a proper newspaper in twenty months so these developments are fresh to my eyes. I just learned that novelist Eric Knight died in a mysterious crash in South America. As a boy I enjoyed his fictions of Lassie. Leslie Howard, the actor, also died. I have so much news to catch up since being a POW. On the bright side, if it weren't for the Curragh I might not be alive now, but I am, and am very grateful. Tomorrow I shall be flying again, only practice flights but at least I'll be in the sky where my dreams have been soaring.

You can send your mail to me at CP, London, Eng. until I learn where I'm to be posted. Can't wait to hear from you. Love to all, *Jack*

P.S. I've been made a Flight-Lieutenant. Nobody knows why. I guess it was my Houdini trick.

Dear Jack, July 15 1943

You got your 'Get Out of Jail Free' card! Yay! I'm happy for you. Now you can return to what you love, flying. I must say, as an RN, I was a bit worried about the suicide attempt until Mother shared Ann's letter with me. I still think you took a huge risk but at least it was under a doctor's supervision, sort of, I guess. Don't ever do that again.

You know by now but I'll tell you myself. I moved to Toronto. Marjorie and I are sharing a little apartment in a rooming house at 41 Madison Ave. We have two bedrooms (thank heaven), a sitting room with two chairs, a wee tiny kitchen with a table and two chairs, an ice box and hot plate, dishes, and a couple of pots. No guests allowed for the first three months until the landlady gets to know what kind of girls we are. She's really very sweet. Dad found her for us through his Anglican connections.

I've been assigned to the Maternity Ward at Toronto General. I've already helped in the birthing of many babies, some born with difficulties. One has a cleft palate and can't suck, making feeding an issue. An experienced nurse showed the mother how to pump her breast milk into a bottle, then raise the bottle above her head onto a shelf, and run a gravity tube from the bottle into the baby's mouth. The baby drinks mother's own and looks straight into her eyes as if she's breast feeding like the others. I tell you, Jack, I may have graduated, but I still have so much to learn, and for the first time in my life, I love learning. There's a point to it all!

Another baby was born with a heart condition. They sent her immediately to Sick Children's Hospital for surgery. Can you believe that? A tiny baby has a cardiologist! Toronto is a wonderful place to work where we see miracles every day. Of course some people die in hospital, it's true, but we do what we can to comfort them in their last hours. I learned a lot from the nuns at St. Joe's in London on that score. They are very compassionate and taught us how to console patients and families.

I wish Dad could be a fly on the wall and see me in uniform, in action. Then maybe I'd get the respect he gives to you boys, and Marjorie. She works in a man's world. What I do is just women's work. One day he'll need a nurse; then he'll know what we're worth. He makes my blood boil.

To change the subject, Mother and Dad were both very interested in your article comparing the Ontario Legislature to the Irish Parliament. Well done! Mother had a copy and we pored over it last weekend. I particularly liked the tone of the piece. You are skilled at making subtle remarks that have a tinge of sarcasm. I can see your wry smile when I read: "The Irishman is essentially a human being who specializes in being more human than most people," written from the point of view of a POW who longs to escape the Curragh prison. And I loved your tight description of Jimmy Masterson's "three mile [swim] to shore in a forty-foot sea the night his Sunderland flying boat came down off the Irish coast, with the loss of nine lives." You tell a story in one sentence. And I suspect you were making a dig when you wrote: "He had a good crack at escaping with some of the rest of us on the night his captain, Flt. Lt. Grant Fleming of Calgary, got clean away." I thought your closing paragraph was perfect: "Now, looking at the barbed wire, Jimmy says sadly: 'This is no place for a fighting man when there's a war on.'" You start out writing about the Irish Parliament and end up making your own political point.

By the way, Mother has received several copies from friends across Canada so you're getting wide coverage thanks to CP. You're really quite famous! Mother has saved a shoebox overflowing with newspaper clippings and letters and telegrams, all about or by you. We're so proud of you, Jack.

Please try to stay safe from now on and come back to us. I'm counting on your lucky star. Love, *Mary xoxo*

Dear Jack, Aug. 2, 1943

Congratulations on your escape. I appreciate Ann's letter. It was indeed helpful to know the circumstances. Mum's the word. To be truthful, your father and I have mixed feelings about your return to service as this means you will be back in the eye of the storm, but we know how devoted you are to the cause and we respect your courage.

Philip is in hospital. Jake sent a telegram that he picked Philip up off the battlefield and carried him to the stretcher area. Thank God they were together. Philip has had surgery to remove shrapnel from his stomach. We received a letter from the Officer of Casualties, and another from the officer in charge of his unit, and yet a third from headquarters. Not very much detail in any of the letters; they just repeat the same news, much the same as the letters we received when you parachuted into Ireland.

I'm finding Philip's injury much harder to cope with, even though it is not too serious. I've been trying to figure out why Philip's has hit me so hard. The only answer I can come up with is that he's my youngest. Also we've had Gerald's sudden death, then your crash, and some days it all seems too much. I have to speak aloud to myself to talk some sense into my head. After all, you three boys are alive.

Mary graduated from nursing in June and moved to Toronto. She has a job at Toronto General Hospital in the maternity wing and she is over the moon. Marjorie won a job with the accounting department of CP in Toronto (thanks to your recommendation) so she and Mary are sharing in a very nice little rooming house on Madison Ave. They seem to have worked out the wrinkles of living together. Mary works the night shift and Marjorie of course has a day job; they're not often awake in the apt. at the same time. I fear they might get on each other's nerves, they're so different; but it's up to them to get along now that they're adults. I have enough on my mind!

I am noticing that most of the young women of the church have found jobs, many of them in industry. The ads sponsoring "Rosie the Riveter" are sporting slogans like "Can you use an electric mixer? If so, you can learn to operate a drill." Many women are building ships, aircraft, cars, trucks, weapons even. The surrounding farms are operated by women. We need more nurses at home because many are flocking overseas. The government is constantly advertising for women to fill the ranks while the men are serving. Those who can't fit into the workforce for a wage are volunteering, donating blood, planting victory gardens, selling war bonds, and canning produce to send over to you boys. I see these shifts and my mind whirls at how fast everything is changing.

Well, Jack dear, here's the end of the aerogramme so I'll sign off. Thinking of you always and praying for your safety. Love, *Mom xo*

Dear Jack, Aug. 4, 1943

Thanks for sending me that fruit basket in hospital. That was a total surprise. I had no address for you as I didn't know where you were posted. I remember a good time with you in the Curragh last year, when we visited the pubs and won a few bob at the racetrack. That was fun.

Mother sent copies of your articles on Ireland. Wow, what a splash! You've made me even more interested in becoming a journalist. You dig in to the history and project your own voice. I thought news was supposed to be relayed dispassionately. Your tone is not fervent but the reader certainly knows where you stand. I've always been keen on history and living history is even better. You tell it as it's happening and that's what I find so appealing. Do you really think you could get me a job after the war? If I could travel as well as write that would be perfect. I'd love to cover the hot spots and inform the folks back home what's happening beyond their back yard. I think Canadians could be more knowledgeable about international affairs, don't you?

My wounds are healing pretty well. I'm stiff and sore from the surgery, but happy that the damage wasn't worse. I'm lucky Jake was posted with the same outfit in Sicily, otherwise I might still be lying face down in the dust. I've been working on physio to strengthen my core and then I'll be heading back to my unit. They're a great bunch of guys. I hope they're all surviving.

I found your article "Thinking Irish Are Uneasy..." particularly fascinating (although there are a few sentences mangled by the copy editor). All along I felt Irish neutrality was a huge mistake, but I understand it better now, and I have more respect for the Irish economy. Their use of peat instead of coal, and their switch from raising cattle to growing wheat were smart choices. Also you point out, "In some village post offices there are long queues when the money comes from 'across the channel' for the soldiers' allowances and workmen's wages." Your conclusion that "Today Éire is better fed and better clothed than any other neutral country in Europe" makes sense. Jack, you know I look up to you and respect your writing very much. I am surprised that you seem to be standing up for the nation that imprisoned you for so long. Your statement "700 years of what Ireland went through cannot be forgotten in 20" converts my sympathy entirely to the neutrality argument. Thanks for mentioning your brothers. I feel almost as famous as you!

Dan Breen's concern that war profiteers from other countries will buy up Irish properties is a valid prediction. It already happened once in Éire's history (when the Horse Protestants somehow acquired all the best land south of the partition). I hope his plan for the Dáil to appropriate all property bought by outside interests during the war is greeted favourably.

Do you know Gillis Purcell? He's a friend of Marjorie's and he works at CP in London now. He dropped in the other day. I guess he promised Marjorie he would. He astounded me with a gift of oranges. He was very hush, hush about where they came from. They sure tasted great after the dust of Italy. Hospital food could not be accused of being nutritious. Whenever I think of the comparative abundance when we grew up, I almost want to cry with shame. We didn't know how good we had it, did we? We've certainly seen another side of life over here.

I could murder a fag at the moment, if they let me have one. I'll sign off for now. Love, *Phil*

Dear Jack,   **Aug. 6, 1943**

Maybe you know by now but I simply must brag that the Conservatives won the Ontario election by a landslide and put the Liberals in their place: 38 seats to 15. And surprise, surprise, those socialists, the CCF, came right up the middle to win status as the Official Opposition with 34 seats. Dad, of course, is tickled pink. Most everyone in the office is still drinking toasts and scribbling stories furiously. Who would have predicted such a stunning victory for George Drew. He'll probably be a great premier, but I think he's a stuffed shirt. He has all the right connections (Upper Canada College, U of T, Osgoode Hall) blah, blah, blah, but I predict he'll start a war with the CCF, whom he calls Reds, and I suspect he's anti-Jewish. In any case, he's pro-British because "they're the right sort of people," and he plans to import loads of them. He has military connections too; he's some sort of WWI hero, now a Lt. Colonel. I don't care about that, to be honest. I voted for him but just because I was sick of the Liberals.

Did you hear that Philip has been wounded in Sicily? Thank heaven Jake was with him and managed to carry him off the field to where the stretcher bearers pick up people and take them away to be treated. He got a stomach full of shrapnel but he'll be okay. Probably not "fighting fit," but he's alive. Mother's been on her knees since she got the telegram. Now there's a more reassuring letter from the casualties' officer that Philip's recovering well. God, I hope so.

I don't know how much news coverage from N. America you read. I know you're awfully busy, so I'll rattle off a few headlines in case you're interested.

We're so proud of our namesake, HMCS Owen Sound, for helping to sink her 3rd submarine.

The Stanley Cup Finals was between the Toronto Maple Leafs and the Detroit Red Wings. In the fourth game, the nail-biter, held in Detroit, the Maple Leafs staved off elimination with a 4–3 victory. Nick Metz scored the winning goal for Toronto with seven minutes to play.

The game ended in a near-riot. In the final minute, Detroit's Eddie Wares drew a misconduct penalty and then a $50 fine. Grosso earned a penalty for too many men on the ice, threw down his stick and gloves and was fined $25 by Harwood. At the end of the game, Detroit coach Jack Adams then attacked Harwood, punching him in the face following a profanity-laced outburst. The fans booed the officiating, littering the ice with paper, peanuts, and even a woman's shoe. NHL president Frank Calder and referee Harwood were escorted out of the rink under police protection. Calder immediately suspended Jack Adams indefinitely and imposed $100 fines on Wares and Grosso.

After losing the first three games, the Maple Leafs won the next four and captured the series 4–3, winning their fourth Stanley Cup. This is the first Stanley Cup Finals in history to go seven games.

The Queen's Plate was held at Woodbine in Toronto, won by Paolita. Strange fact: Paolita's time was 2:02:60 while last year's winner, Ten to Ace's time was 1:57:80, and 1941 winner, Budpath's time was 1:56:80, and 1940 winner, Willie the Kid's time was 1:55:80. Are you noticing a pattern? Each year the winner is slower. What's with that? Gotta love the horses' names, eh.

On the bright side I've seen two movies lately that you might like if you have a chance. *Heart of the Golden West* with Roy Rogers and Gabby Hayes was terrific, for a Western. *Girl Crazy* with Mickey Rooney and Judy Garland, "a fast stepping musical comedy," was terrific in anybody's books. You should take Ann to see that one.

You would notice a lot of changes in Toronto. It is now a major military centre. Exhibition Place I is a training hub. The Island Airport has been seconded by the RCAF and the Royal Norwegian Air Force. Civilian manufacturing companies, such as Inglis, have been converted to production of armaments. At Malton and Downsview Airports new aviation factories are building fighters and bombers. I see uniforms on the streetcars and buses all the time.

Mary moved in with me at the beginning of summer. It's great to share the rent with someone who's actually earning more than I am. My CP pay as a clerk with no U education is not that wonderful. Mary's pay is not top-notch either being as she's just starting out, but between the two of us, we make rent plus enough for groceries and other stuff. She works shift so we're not usually awake at the same time, which gives us each free time in our very small kitchen. Whenever her boyfriend stops by to pick her up, he seems to fill the whole place. I like him; he's a big tease and loads of fun. Mary told me to stop flirting with him. Hey, I'm innocent!

Well, dear brother, I hope you get to sleep in your own bed from now on. Don't be too cocky for a while. Mother couldn't take another shock just yet. Dad's coping okay but he's showing his age. I know you gotta do what you gotta do, but I'm praying you'll come out of this smelling like a rose again. I'm counting on your own saying: "the things that go wrong then right again."

I'm doing well, loving the folks in the office. Can't wait until we're both working full time with CP, me in Toronto, you in London. Love, *Marjorie*

Dear Mom and Dad,   **Aug. 16, 1943**

By now you will have received official word that I am in hospital after a crash. Tomorrow I am being moved from Fusehill Military Hospital in Carlisle to East Grinstead, the famous Queen Vic Hospital. A top surgeon is flying north to treat me. I do have a broken jaw, four teeth missing, a gash from my forehead to my chin, plus a bit of a burn on my face, all of which can be fixed. I'm enjoying beer through a straw as my main source of nutrition.

Friends are beginning to dribble northward to visit when they have leave and they are a wonderful source of amusement, or rather, I am a source of amusement for them as they can't get over how I rearranged my face to attract the nurses. I also banged up my left leg, a compound fracture, apparently repaired with plates; the cast is rather annoying when I try to sit down in the very small toilet cubicles here. They say the leg will be right as rain in 8 weeks. I doubt that the war will be lost for lack of my humble service, but 8 weeks does seem a long time from where I'm lying in a wee hospital gown.

The crash happened during an all-night practice run. The Anson began to fall in cloud, as if out of control. I went forward and the captain apparently got the A/C under control, then put the nose down to avoid another huge patch of cloud. I started back to the 1st navigator to see about our position and safety height. That is the last I recall until I woke up in hospital at Carlisle.

I've just become aware of another story. I might have died from shock and exposure had it not been for the heroic actions of a nurse and her boyfriend. They hiked 10 miles up Green Gable Hill in Northern England to the wreckage, administered first aid, and were responsible for carrying me out of there.

Now I am progressing favourably from "dangerously ill" to "seriously ill." You see how fast I am recovering and what good care I am receiving.

To be honest I actually requested, nay begged, to go on this flight as I had had no night flying experience in two years. As Aesop would say, "Be careful what you wish for."

Could you please send me some juice packs (those Cana pressers are tasty)? I doubt the postal service would approve sending beer. My visitors are bringing gallons of it anyway, enough to share around the ward.

I want to tell you how brave some of these lads really are. I have helped the nurses hold down a bumptious Ontario rear gunner, as he came down from under the anesthetic after an operation leading to the building of new tissue about the nose. He has been the sole survivor of bomber crashes twice, and still he is begging to go back into service.

I have seen a Canadian airman wheeled in badly burned after crash-landing his four-engine aircraft, which he brought back from Germany on two engines, and then I have heard his nurses whisper, 'He wants to know if he will be flying again in a month.' No one could help feeling the spirit that permeates this place.

Each week members of the RCAF Women's Division, at their own expense and of their own free will, come from London with cigarettes, candy and comforts for the men.

I can say with confidence that my convalescence will be a very luxurious one. I even found an old typewriter that wasn't seeing any use in the administrative office, so I'm all set.

I do hope you both are in good health and spirits. Please tell Marjorie and Mary that the war is nearly over. I'm hearing very positive reports from the lads who are seeing the action from a front row seat. Let me know when you hear news of Jake or Phil. I'll write again soon. Love to all, *Jack*

My Dear Son,   **Aug. 20, 1943**

My soul is at ease now that you have survived yet another crash. You must still be carrying the rabbit foot in your pocket.

I remember the day you brought it home with pride and your mother discovered it while she was going through pockets before washing the clothes. I believe she threw out the rabbit foot and you retrieved it from the garbage. You carried it around like a sacred talisman for years. Do you still have it?

Your setback is unfortunate but you are in the prime of life and I am confident you will recover to full health and strength in time. God's hand in healing is part of His work as Creator. Soon you'll be back on the road to energy and happiness.

We have the most amazing news to tell you. Churchill himself met with FDR here in Quebec City. The announcement of the completion of the conference, with pictures, has just come out in all the papers. Mr. Mackenzie King looks like the cat that swallowed the canary. Nobody even knew that the dignitaries were in Canada, except of course those in the need to know. What a huge honour for our country to be selected as the conference to go down in history! I wonder what plans were set afoot in those rooms of La Citadelle du Québec.

We've had a rather nasty election campaign here in Ontario. George Drew is calling the CCF party a bunch of communists, "Reds" to be exact, just because they stand for equal wages, mother's allowance, equal land ownership, etc. They fight for farmer's rights, workers of all kinds, and miners too. Someone has to stand up for the little guy; the bottom rung in a capitalist society suffers unjustifiably.

Our nickel has been devalued. Five-cent coins, which actually contain an alloy of copper, silver, and manganese, don't contain nickel at all, because it's being saved for the war effort. Coin collectors will be in their glory.

I have one other tidbit to share with you and then I really must go to bed. It's been a long day of visiting very sad folks. One widow has now lost all three of her sons. Another lost the father of her new baby. But I don't want to bring you down with stories of sorrow. Actually the bravery of these two women, one older, one younger, moved me deeply. Neither is giving in to despair.

I'll tell you of an intriguing discovery: an engraving found on a tree in the Bruce Trail that says: "Poland has not yet perished. This soldier will help." It must have been carved by one of the soldiers stationed in Owen Sound for a short time; we told you about them.

Do you know that Canada's famed Great War flying ace, Billy Bishop, hails from Owen Sound? Even though you weren't born here, you can probably relate to him. He is quite the storyteller too.

We were so pleased to hear from your friend Ann. She certainly sounds like someone you'd want to have in your corner during a fight. I think she's splendid.

Now I must say goodnight to you, my dear Jack. Love, *Dad*

Dear Jack,   **Sep. 29, 1943**

I simply had to write to you when I heard about your crash. I told you I'm counting on your lucky star. Your injuries sound rather serious, especially your broken jaw and facial burns. Yikes! You must be quite a sight for Ann.

This photograph, taken at Inverhuron Beach, shows the man I'm dating. His name is Lindsay Mason, from Stratford. You might remember him from our summers there when we were kids. At least you should remember his older sisters, Dorothy, Betty, and Ruth. They are closer to your age.

He is home on leave as a navigator with RCAF and his sister, Ruth just had a baby in the maternity ward in Toronto where I am working. He wanted to see her, and her husband is still overseas, so Lindsay lied and said he was his sister's husband. Get it? Only husbands are allowed into our ward.

Lindsay asked me on a date and I said no. I set him up with 3 different nurses, all of whom he dated, but he kept asking me. I thought of him as that brat from Inverhuron; besides, he's three years younger than I am. Who wants a man who's younger? Anyway, he sure is persistent.

I finally told him I would go on one date, just one, just bowling. As you know, I'm a pretty good bowler, so I cleaned his clock, but his manhood wasn't insulted at all. I thought if he could take a good hiding by a woman maybe he'd be okay husband material. Besides, we clicked. He is one big flirt, and sort of stuck on himself in a confident swagger sort of way so he'll probably be able to make some sort of career for himself, although he has no idea what he wants to do.

His sisters all had university educations. Then along came the war and he signed up. Now there's no family money left for university for Lindsay. He might go into insurance or the bank. They provide courses.

Did I mention that he's drop-dead handsome? Well, you can see for yourself. We drove his father's car up to the beach for a day picnic. Marjorie came too, with a girlfriend. Do you remember Dorcas? She works in the Bank of Commerce and might get Lindsay an introduction after he comes home from the war. He returns to duty next Sunday.

That's enough about me. How are you, Jack? I hope they keep you in hospital for a long time until you're good and ready to resume flying. How often do you and Ann see each other? How do you keep yourself sorted? I imagine fighting a war is exhausting and emotionally draining, and so is being in love. You're on a real roller coaster.

Do you remember this poem from school? I really like the line "danced the skies on laughter-silvered wings." That's how I think of you. Love, *Mary xoxo*

"High Flight" by John Gillespie Magee

> Oh! I have slipped the surly bonds of Earth
> And danced the skies on laughter-silvered wings;
> Sunward I've climbed, and joined the tumbling mirth
> of sun-split clouds,—and done a hundred things
> You have not dreamed of—wheeled and soared and swung
> High in the sunlit silence. Hov'ring there,
> I've chased the shouting wind along, and flung
> My eager craft through footless halls of air....

Up, up the long, delirious, burning blue
I've topped the wind-swept heights with easy grace
Where never lark nor ever eagle flew—
And, while with silent lifting mind I've trod
The high untrespassed sanctity of space,
Put out my hand, and touched the face of God.

Dear Mom and Dad,　　　　　　　　　　　Oct. 10, 1943

Good news to report concerning my recovery: the hospital's chief surgeon, Dr. A. H. McIndoe, has completed a skin graft on my face. It is the most remarkable surgery. They take a piece of my own skin from inside my thigh and patch it onto my cheek. The operation went very well and the graft is taking. One more surgery like that and I'll be as good as new. I suffered a concussion, and lacerations and burns to my face but the doc assures me that the scars will fade with applications of vitamin E cream. I think I look a bit older, and certainly feel wiser!

I'm walking too, with a slight limp, but working on increasing my distance every day. The cast just came off so the leg is weak, not used to being without that support. I asked Doc McIndoe when the limp will go away. His answer: "When you stop limping!" I'm finding that a challenge, but when I see the other lads working hard to regain their strength in order to get back in the game, I'm inspired. Dad, you're preaching the miracle of creation; well, I'm experiencing the miracle of re-creation. The body is an amazing machine. I am grateful that I did not lose my leg, or my eye.

Ann has stood by me through everything. She truly is a remarkable girl. She's smart and funny, doesn't let me get away with whining, and always encourages me. I'm enclosing a picture for you to see for yourselves how beautiful she is. She's rather shy about that, but I think you'll agree: she's striking. Of course you can tell that I'm smitten. And here's the great part: I've asked her to marry me when the war is over and she said yes! You will have at least one daughter-in-law, and we're hoping for lots of babies, so you will have grandchildren to dance on your knees.

I can picture you coming to England to help tend the little ones and tour the countryside to see all the lovely towns where I've spent my leaves. You see, I had to sign a pact when I left the Curragh that I would never write again. It was forced on me by the Canadian High Commissioner, so it only applies to Canada. Apparently my articles had become an embarrassment to Ireland (no surprise). I will be able to make a living here, so that's the plan. My pension from the RAF combined with salary as a foreign correspondent will be enough for a comfortable living, so Ann and I will certainly visit Canada frequently too. Transatlantic flights will become common in the future.

Last week, before my cast was removed, a medical orderly took me off the hospital grounds for the first time. As he swung the wheelchair down the drive and out towards the street, I realized that circumstances can make even a wheelchair ride exciting — though it would require a strong imagination indeed to relate it to flying. We had only gone a few yards and I was absorbing the warm sunlight when the orderly stopped and pointed to the field on our right.

"That's where the Canadian wing is going to be," he said.

Then I heard for the first time of plans for a hospital unit which will bring to badly burned and injured Canadian airmen the finest treatment that the miracles of modern surgery can offer. Many men of the RCAF and RAF already have been spared the tragedy of having to go the remainder of life terribly scarred or maimed.

A great majority of the servicemen who have come here, many of them all the way from the front in the Middle East, have returned to active duty. None has gone away hopeless. Dr. McIndoe told me that when the facilities are finished, the Canadian wing will have no equal in the world. The 50-bed unit may never be completely filled with Canadian patients, although it is to be primarily for the RCAF cases requiring plastic surgery on jaw treatment. Beds left available will be turned over to other war casualties.

Regular visits of stage and screen entertainers from London are a part of the hospital program now. Two weeks ago I shook the hand of Vera Lynn. As she toured the wards she spent time with each of us. She showed genuine interest in where we were from and what had brought us here. She even graced us with a spontaneous mini-concert and sang favourites of the patients. The ones I remember are: "The White Cliffs of Dover," "A Nightingale Sang in Berkeley Square," and "We'll Meet Again." Trust me, there wasn't a dry eye in the house when she finished. Her last number was, "There'll Always Be an England" and everyone who was able stood. The pianist had tears streaming down his face as he watched us. What a motley crew we must have appeared, bandages and crutches and wheelchairs, but eyes shining with hope.

I've been very busy with treatments and exercises and hospital routine and find little time for writing but know that you are in my heart every hour. I am so grateful for the life you have given me.

Thank you for the fruit juices, jellies, crackers, and sardines. They make me think of home and you. Love to all, *Jack*

Miss Ann Mitchell, only daughter of Major C. C. Mitchell, D.S.O., M.C., of Ballynure, Co. Wicklow, is a member of the W.R.N.S. Her father is joint Master of the Kildare Hounds with Sir Francis Brooke, Bt.

Dear Jack,   Oct. 12, 1943

Congrats on your engagement! Everyone here at CP sends their best wishes. Mom is all excited about the prospect of a wedding in Ireland after the war. Maybe she'll look up her long lost cousin in Co. Clare. Mary and I won't be able to come to the wedding, naturally, but depending on the date, maybe Jake and Phil can be with you to represent the family. In any case, your many friends here in the office will miss a grand party. Maybe we'll buy a bottle of Irish whiskey to share on the big day, raise a glass each and tell a "Jack story."

Gillis Purcell is very sorry to lose you as his star foreign correspondent. What is that all about? He asked me for the inside scoop at Friday afternoon drinks and I had to confess that I haven't a clue. He's hoping "a good wife" will talk some sense into you and change your mind. CP stocks will go down if you don't come back to the fold. Never write again for Canada? Impossible.

Too bad you tore up the book on Irish history. But you know what they say: the second manuscript will be better. You're not the first writer to lose a brain child. Remember that story about Hemingway's suitcase? At the time he was covering the Lausanne Peace Conference for the *Toronto Daily Star* where he met some big NY editor he wanted to impress. Hadley, his wife, packed up every piece of writing she could find in their Paris apartment to bring to him in Switzerland. Unfortunately she lost the suitcase at the train station.

After the loss of his early work some say he changed his style to the strong, lean writing that made him famous. Very disciplined and spare. Are you a fan of Hemingway? I read his collection of stories and I'll never forget "The Short Happy Life of Francis Macomber." Many reporters around the office say, "I'm still drinking their whisky," but I don't think they use that phrase properly. They say it after a great interview instead of after a crappy one; though they like the reference to whisky.

This letter is short. Just had to congratulate you and Ann on your engagement. You'll be the first of the five of us to marry. (It sounds weird to say "five of us," leaving out Gerald. We've always thought of the six of us.)

"There is nothing to writing. All you do is sit down at a typewriter and bleed."

Keep your shorts clean. Love, *Marjorie*

Dear Jack,   Oct. 18, 1943

Congratulations on your engagement! The family are all thrilled for you both. I went home last weekend for a couple of days off and saw Ann's photograph. Mother has it in a little silver frame on the mantel, place of honour. No doubt it will also serve as a happy topic of conversation when she hosts visitors. You are a lucky man, Jack. Mother shared Ann's letter with me and we picked it apart for clues to her character. She certainly sounds wonderful and she will be good for you. We have to think about living, about life after Hitler.

As for you, it's a funny time to ask a girl to marry you when you can't even kneel down and do it properly. What about a ring? When I become engaged I want a ring. It's not official for a girl until there's a ring on her finger, so you'd better figure out a way for that to happen. And I want to hear all about that proposal too.

Jack, I'm so happy that you survived your latest crash. You've always landed on your feet and been lucky, but this time you really frightened us. If you were suffering from exposure as well as all your injuries, you were darn lucky that a nurse found you. She must have had a first aid kit and she knew exactly what to do: clean the wounds, splint the leg, wrap the head, and build a stretcher. Ten miles is quite a journey if you're carrying 160 extra pounds. She and her boyfriend deserve medals.

Working in a hospital every day we see all kinds. The emergency room is the worst ward, in my opinion. Many of the casualties are victims of drunk driving, or stupid driving, or thoughtless driving. I've never seen a person with your particular combination of injuries, but I have seen lots of compound fractures with leg bones exposed, and I've seen cases of lost teeth, especially in sports. I'm glad you didn't explain too much to Mother and Father. Of course I realized right away that you must have been in extreme pain at the beginning of your recovery. You're putting on a brave face and I hope that means you're doped up with pain killers, besides beer, I mean.

Well, for a boy from small-town Ontario you sure do lead an exciting life! It's not too, too surprising that you'll be living abroad with Ann. We all understand the circumstances, but it must be said, we'll miss you terribly at home. Your letters mean such a lot to Mother and Father. Marjorie and I read them too. You could write a book, ha ha!

All my best love, *Mary xoxo*

Dear Jack and Ann,   Oct. 20, 1943

We are so happy for you both. Ann, dear, welcome to the family. Even though you will be living in England I hope we will stay close through letters and lots of photographs of those future little Calders. I would be delighted to fly across the pond to babysit as long as you promise to cook up a batch of good old Irish stew.

You two are already proving what strong partners you are for each other. Jack, your escape from the Curragh would not have been possible without Ann's collaboration, as I'm sure you know. She played a vital part in securing her family doctor's advice for the dangerous escapade.

I must confess my heart stopped when I read the account of the iodine experiment. Thank goodness for modern medicine and good friends like Mr. Girdlestone. His timely intervention probably saved your life. Is he still in prison?

Now the two of you have another challenge. Ann, I am so grateful that you are there by Jack's side during his recuperation. Mental and emotional health are important as well as physical in the healing process, and that's where you can help Jack. He speaks of you in glowing terms and I sense that he loves you deeply. Never before has he written to me about a girl in his life so I know you are very special to him. I treasure you for loving my boy and look forward to the day when I may call you daughter-in-law.

Jack, you've asked for word of Jake and Phil. All I know is that I had birthday telegrams from them in April and a Happy Thanksgiving message recently from Phil. Jake wrote a very short letter describing a young woman named Betty he plans to bring home after he gets out of the service. She sounds lovely.

Thank you for the picture of Ann. It makes such a difference to have a face to go with a name. She has a strong look about her as well as beautiful features. Be good to her, Jack.

As for me, somehow I have become Director of the Board of Education. Your father fulfilled the role admirably in Chatham and he advised me to take up the post. When the sticky bits come along, and they will surely raise their ugly heads, I will be able to turn to him for guidance. I just started chairing the board in September and my calendar is already full of committee meetings. The immediate problem is a shortage of qualified teachers, especially in the one-room rural schools. I'm afraid standards are being lowered and we are forced to accept any willing individual who wants a salary and can cope with children as a means to that end. Interviews are ongoing as some people quit after a few weeks of pranks passed down from wayward uncles. Summer courses to train teachers are the short-term solution but even they are not churning out the numbers fast enough. We simply must take younger candidates and train them on the job with supplementary night courses. The older teachers who did not qualify for service overseas are run off their feet tutoring the younger ones as well as coping with larger classes themselves. Still, we carry on.

I must close for tonight. Everyone sends best wishes. You are in my thoughts and prayers. May this war end soon so that we can all carry on with the normal, happy business of living.

Love to you both, *Mom xo*

Dear Jack,   Nov. 30, 1943

How is your recovery? I do hope you are not in pain now that your leg is healing. You never said what happened with your teeth. Do you have a partial plate, a bridge? I hope your surgeon is able to do something about the left side of your mouth; otherwise you'll be looking lopsided down the road. (You're not too old to take advice from your mother!)

You were right about the challenges of being Director of the Board of Ed. Since I took over the reins in September, a few, very few actually, parents are bringing complaints to our sessions that the school yards are overrun with children playing war games, bringing homemade guns and helmets and all manner of trappings and scaring other children. The war is not here but it creeps into our daily lives in so many insidious ways. The radios proclaim news from the front in every home and children are there with their eager ears, ready to imitate their heroes. I tell the parents, "It's only natural for children to play 'bad guy/good guy.' It happens in every generation, no matter the scenario."

In my new role as Director I'm also being exposed to racism that disturbs me. Some Jewish parents are complaining that their children are being bullied. And, here in Owen Sound, the few Negro children are teased mercilessly. In Chatham, because we lived at the top of the Underground Railroad, our children grew up playing together and nobody noticed any difference. I find it remarkable that a few miles away, in Owen Sound, different attitudes fester. Of course the racism starts with the parents, but how to address it, is my concern.

Our teachers need helpful policies to discipline such situations before they get out of hand entirely. I read recently that the New York actor Marlon Brando was expelled from school for riding a motorcycle through the corridors. I hope I don't have to deal with anything that extreme! It would be a case of popularity ruling the day, I fear. On the other hand, one cannot discipline innocent children to the extent that we come down too harshly on their natural instincts to create play from the adult world they see every day, as long as it doesn't hurt another child. I think I'm ranting! Sorry.

Your father felt very proud to attend the commissioning of HMCS Owen Sound this month. Do you remember that we told you she was being built over the winter in Collingwood? Your father received a very nice invitation, all embossed, very fancy.

It amuses me that war ships are called "she" and "flower." I think it shows that some tenderness lurks beneath the surface of even the toughest of men. I know the tender heart of each of my sons and my husband, but you boys are special, aren't you!

Jack, you have been very brave through your ordeals, first being in prison for so long, and now your service being put on hold again with hospitalization. I'm your mother; I can read between the lines. I know how disappointed you must be these days, waiting for another chance to join the action. I know you're anxious to be back with the lads; you didn't sign up to watch the game. Your turn will come. Do you remember Milton's poem? He's asking God if his blindness will deny him a role, and the reply comes:

> "God doth not need
> Either man's work or his own gifts; who best
> Bear his mild yoke, they serve him best. His state
> Is Kingly: Thousands at his bidding speed
> And post o'er land and ocean without rest;
> They also serve who only stand and wait."[viii]

As a mother, I've always loved that last line. Not that I "only stand and wait," but I've often felt that life was passing me by while I washed dishes and clothes and floors and everyone else was involved to the hilt. Now I have a chance to use my brain and maybe develop some leadership, and guess what? I miss all the hustle and noise and chaos of six children under my feet. What I'm trying to say, Jack dear, is take this time of convalescence to think about your next move and write your reflections of East Grinstead. It reputes to be an amazing place of healing.

You know I don't regret any of the stages of my life. Even though I resist moving from one place to another, after it's over and I've settled in, I enjoy meeting new people and getting to know another community. I think a change gives one perspective. I hope you have time to ponder what you can learn from your crash, dear Jack. Love, *Mom xo*

Dear Jack,   Dec. 14, 1943

Your mother and I are decorating the house for Christmas and we can't help but think of you boys as we open the boxes and the memories pour out. Remember that year that you got a Meccano set and Jake got a chemistry set and Philip was jealous because he only got a little red wagon that wouldn't "do anything" until the snow melted? He nearly set the house on fire when you weren't looking. We were alerted when smoke began pouring up the basement stairs into the kitchen. Baking soda saved the day. Philip was always trying to catch up to his older brothers but of course that was impossible. You were his guardians, when you weren't trying to ditch him for some tom foolery of your own.

That was the year Char was hit by a car. She had a great life, following you children everywhere on your adventures. In this instance she was chasing your bikes and a car sideswiped her. The whole family was upset for days but that little Spaniel only suffered bruising and recovered without surgery. In a family of eight there's always someone who could use a cuddle with a gentle dog. She certainly enjoyed lots of brushing and lived for sixteen years.

When we adopted Char we already had Spook. She was not amused when Char wanted to play. Remember the Christmas kittens that surprised us? Your mother and I were trying to figure out what year that was. Spook chose to give birth in the linen closet so your mother was alarmed, but we found a box and soon the wee family was comfortable in the kitchen near the stove. Various members of the parish graciously adopted the kittens in February and we were rewarded with cat stories ever after.

One year your Aunt Madge and Uncle Joe drove from Windsor for Christmas. They had a flat tire en route and were late arriving, then drank a year's worth of sherry and slept most of the day away on the 24th. Of course, they had lots of pointers for my sermon and were rather disappointed to hear my version.

Do you remember that everyone was fed up with listening to their critique when finally, Gerald, who wouldn't say "Boo" to a goose, said, "Go suck eggs?" Goodness only knows where he picked up such a quaint expression. How we laughed!

The little crèche is safely ensconced on the mantel over the fireplace. Even though Mary and Joseph wouldn't have known a pine tree in their lives, I cut some fresh pine boughs to drape around it. Mother likes the scent in the house at Christmas, and so do I. Mary and Marjorie are coming on the weekend to help finish with the decorating and baking. They enjoy the big kitchen here as theirs is tiny. Philip is back in action. He and Jake will be on a battlefield in Italy for Christmas.

Your mother and I join with your sisters in wishing you and Ann a Merry Christmas, dear boy. I don't know if you will be together as perhaps she will go back to Ireland to be with her parents. Your mother mailed a care package early to make sure it arrives on time. I am instructed to tell you to open it with Ann. I think your mother packed it with the two of you in mind. It seems odd to wish someone to be merry in hospital. E. Grinstead, however, sounds more like a rehabilitation healing place. We hope you will have a church service, special music, and a lovely meal. Our blessings upon you. Love, *Dad*

Part Four

1944

Dear Jack, Jan. 27, 1944

Thanks for the birthday telegram. Very exciting to receive a cable on one's birthday. And guess what else I received? Yes, Lindsay popped the question, down on one knee and everything. Totally romantic.

Lindsay gave me a ring. It's a beautiful diamond set in white gold on a yellow gold band. There are 2 little shoulder diamonds. It really sparkles! Lindsay picked it out himself. You'll never believe this story. A doctor, named Lance Stirrett, who is engaged to Lindsay's sister Betty, came around the ward selling diamond rings from a briefcase! Isn't that the strangest? If it were anyone else, we wouldn't know whether to trust that the diamond is genuine, but Lance is marrying into the family, so he wouldn't cheat his own brother-in-law, would he?

I heard from Mother that you did buy Ann a ring after all, a sapphire. I guess she wouldn't want an emerald if she's "leaving Ireland forever." If you chose her ring, I'm sure it's really gorgeous. You are a classy guy and have good taste.

Mom's head is spinning too at the thought of three family weddings, yours, Jake's, and now mine. Dad and I are arguing about the vows. He insists that I have to say the words "and obey." I tell him that Lindsay's and my relationship is not like that but he won't listen. He sure is a chauvinist at times. Is Ann going to say "and obey?" What do you think about that? After all that women have contributed to the war effort you'd think we finally earned the right to step out of the kitchen. Mom's Chair of the Board of Ed. for crying out loud. The days of women "obeying" husbands are long gone.

O Jack, I'm so happy for us all. Everyone says we've already beaten Hitler. We're impatient for the announcement. We know you boys are working non-stop to bring about Victory. There will be dancing in the streets when the Germans finally surrender. Please take care until then. Love, *Mary xoxo*

Dear Mary,   **February 10, 1944**

Congratulations to you and Lindsay on your engagement! Ann sends her best wishes along too. We hope you will enjoy every happiness and you certainly seem to be bubbling over with it already. Lindsay is a lucky guy. I hope he knows what a treasure you are, my dear sis. You have such a big heart, to go with that pretty face; it's no wonder he fell in love on the spot. I sort of remember him from our wild youth at Inverhuron. He was a bratty kid, after all. You didn't pay much attention to him then, did you? Maybe you flirted!

Ann and I have had no time for wedding plans. Of course the ceremony will have to be held back in Ireland in her folks' parish church. Her parents were very kind to me when I was a POW. I was invited to their home many times, including Christmas of '42. I don't think Ann would have any trouble saying the words "and obey" in her vows because she knows how much I respect her and that I would never hold her to my opinion just because I'm the alpha male. Still, I shall bring up the topic with her and who knows, she might surprise me.

The story of how Lindsay acquired your wedding ring is indeed a shocker. Your future brother-in-law, Lance, sounds like a bit of a charlatan! I don't think doctors are licensed to sell rings from a briefcase to nurses' boyfriends. Why not have that ring examined at your local Birks store? If it turns out to be glass, Lindsay can warn his sister and retrieve a refund from Lance. Am I sounding like too much of an older brother? I don't mean to take away from your big moment.

I bet Mom and Dad are happy for you too. I'm sorry Dad is insisting on your saying "and obey." It's tradition and he is, after all, a man of his time. On your side, I know you would take your vows very seriously. We were always taught that words matter; one's word is one's bond and all that. Stand up for yourself, sis. I'll have a word in his ear too if you like.

Marjorie hasn't met anyone yet, has she? If so, she's being awfully quiet about it. Now that you two are living together, you probably know what's going on in her life, so do tell me.

I saw Philip in hospital last summer. Gosh, it seems like yesterday. He doesn't have anyone special and seemed to be enjoying the attention from the nurses. He's still young, after all.

You would be really impressed with the layout of Queen Victoria Hospital, E. Grinstead. Along with the surgical wards, there are cottages for patients who are in rehabilitation, where I live now. I have benefitted from burn care, eye and jaw surgery, orthodontics, leg surgery, and physiotherapy; you name it, I've done the rounds of nearly all the wards. There is a new wing planned for Canadian casualties that will be state-of-the-art. I regularly tour the Peanut ward for children and am always inspired by the courage and playfulness of its patients. They cheer me up. As I was on a liquid diet for months I also spend time in the "Guinea Pig Pub," a nod to my surgeon, Dr. McIndoe's, sense of humour. The place is fairly brimming with positive vibes, important in the healing process.

I am very happy that you have hit your stride in the maternity ward. That's the perfect spot for you. I was quite touched by your letter concerning the names of the boys whom we have lost to the war, names I remember from school. On the one hand, many are dying; on the other, many are born. At least you get to experience joy during these years of famine. Gerald would be proud of you. Life has a funny way of balancing, don't you agree?

Say, the next time you're home for the weekend, would you do me a favour? Dig out Gerald's diary and copy a few of his poems for me? That would be swell. I'm trying to remember the one he wrote about the stars; you know the one. Love, *Jack*

WOUNDED CANADIANS GIVEN FINEST OF SURGICAL CARE

(Flt. Lt. Jack Calder, of Goderich and Chatham, and former Sports Editor of the Chatham Daily News and Canadian Press staff writer, now an observer with the R.C.A.F., was seriously injured about the face and in one knee some time ago in an air crash. His injuries were treated at the plastic surgery and jaw injuries centre at the Queen Victoria Hospital at East Grinstead, Sussex. He has written this story now that the cure is almost complete.)

BY FLT. LT. JACK CALDER

EAST GRINSTEAD, Sussex, Dec. 11.—The medical orderly swung the wheelchair down the drive and out towards the street. It was my first venture from ward three and, as we moved from the shadows of the hospital buildings, I realized that circumstances can make even a wheelchair ride exciting — though it would require a strong imagination indeed to relate it to flying.

We had only gone a few yards and I was absorbing the warm sunlight when the orderly stopped and pointed to the field on our right.

"That's where the Canadian wing is going to be," he said.

Then I heard for the first time of plans for a hospital unit which will bring to badly burned and in-

FLT.-LT. JACK CALDER

Dear Mom and Dad, Feb. 15, 1944

How are you both? Thank you for your letter to Ann. Your warmth meant a great deal to her. She spends all her free time

with me in E. Grinstead. We go for long walks (at least they're long for me!) and usually end up taking our supper in the village.

This is a small market town with many half-timber buildings covered in ivy, very picturesque. Known as the Town with a Heart, there are volunteer women on the street greeting everyone in a uniform, no matter how scarred or disfigured, myself included. The cynic thinks that the women are husband-hunting, but I've seen with my own eyes that they don't latch on; they greet everyone equally, and will spend time talking to any serviceman who needs a friend. Over a cuppa, they offer to write letters home, especially if the lad is wondering how to tell the folks about the extent of his injuries.

Ann and I rented a car and took a wee holiday in Scotland. Enclosed is a photo she snapped of me for you at Dumfries. You see how well I have recovered. On the way home we drove past Green Gable Hill, the site of my crash, and hiked up to the very spot. The remains of the wreckage are still there. Very sobering. Did I tell you that Willie Panasik, whom we all knew very well, a top-notch pilot, bought the farm in that accident, as did another crew member? I was lucky to survive. Ann and I said a prayer in the Anglican Church. The clock tower with a town bell that used to strike the Angelus still rings the curfew at 5:30. What a lovely tradition.

Bobby Keefer came to see me. He took the train up from London and brought a six-pack of Newcastle brown, so we sat and sipped our way through the afternoon (Keefer, 245–50). He finally got permission to come back to the big show from his long sojourn in Canada. He is flying photo reconnaissance to capture the images of the targets before and the damages after missions. He flies a Mosquito, one of the fastest aircraft out there; and it can fly super high. Both these features make it one of the safest. Bobby thinks that his former boss, whom he calls "the old man," arranged this assignment for him. He was awarded the DFC, but he is very modest about it, as if we all should have won one. Fleming, a squadron leader now, is flying out of the same aerodrome, Benson, so they see a lot of each other. I am hoping to get back to flying ops with them. Bobby had so many questions that the afternoon flew by until he had to leave. I was sorry to see him go.

He and Fleming are two of the bravest men I know. They don't have to keep coming back after so many missions but they are full of passion to complete the purpose for which we signed up. It's hard to explain why, once having experienced the risk and felt the danger firsthand, they don't want to go home. They know that this war won't be won by backing away when the job is nearly done; we have to see it through to the finish. The war in Europe is almost won and we all want to be a part of the final victory. Morale in the RAF is very high at the moment.

The trip to Scotland, especially the hiking, showed me that the leg is practically ready for active service. I feel hale and hearty. My face has healed almost completely. I eat regular food now. I still have a few scars but so does everyone. Ann says they enhance my smile. I think I have a dimple I didn't used to have. "Quirky" is the word she uses. Who knows what she means by that!

In the next few days I'll find out my post. I'm actually itching for the action, the comradery, the sense of purpose in each day. Write soon. Love to all, *Jack*

Dear Mom and Dad, March 1, 1944

I've been deemed fit for service again. I'm excited to get back in the action; I want to be part of the push into Europe. We know we've won the air war but Hitler is pounding the Eastern front on his way to Russia. I think he's making a big mistake, dividing his forces on both fronts. He's opening the door to losing the war.

Jake is very busy with the campaign in Italy from what I hear, so don't worry if you haven't heard from him. His living conditions are not the most conducive to letter writing. His commanding officer, Field Marshall Montgomery, "Monty" they call him, is known to be "unbeatable and unbearable." He has two dogs, one named Hitler and the other named Rommel. I think Jake is in good hands with Princess Patricia's in the new Canadian Corps as long as he keeps his nose clean. Remember "Jake and His Gravediggers?" What a name for a band! Dad, did you find it embarrassing? I don't think Jake would get too far trying that sarcasm on Monty.

I've been in London for a few days, having a medical and touching base with my bosses. I also dropped in to the CP office to see the staff and thank them for the support in getting my articles sent on the wire to Canada. Of course we spent time kidding around. They all think I'm operating 100% even though I look older (so do they, but I bit my tongue).

Writing has really kept me sane these past eight months in hospital. Recuperation is pretty boring business and I am grateful to have had some purpose through it all.

I dropped in to the Brevit Club, hoping to see Bobby and Fleming and some of the others. Wow, what a welcome they gave me! Everyone stood up and cheered and raised their glasses. A very humbling moment. Man, it was good to see their faces and hear their crazy banter and stories. There's a lot to be said for sharing a few brew with your friends and cheering about something happy. You know, Mom and Dad, I think my scars instilled hope that we're going to pull through together.

Of course Ann was with me. Bobby has a new girlfriend named Mary Oldfield, who develops the films he takes. Whenever he delivers them to her, he arrives with flowers. Fleming was with his Irish colleen who came to England to be with him. They aim to own a ranch in Saskatchewan and raise cattle and horses one day. The six of us will see a lot of each other whenever we can. We've even planned a reunion in Co. Kildare, home of the Curragh.

Unfortunately Command is not sending me to Benson to fly in the same squadron as Bobby and Fleming, but because I performed very well in training, I'll be serving in an elite crew, flying a Mossie PR.XVI, one of the fastest and highest flying machines in the air. It looks as though I may get a real break this time. I took one up for a test drive and was it ever formidable! Maxes out at 30,000 feet, maybe higher. The Germans have only one fighter that surpasses it, and not too many of those. Our job will be to fly ahead of the main force of bombers to mark targets, so we have the element of surprise as well as speed.

My new address will be Unit 8, Squadron 571, Oakington, England. I'll be back in London in two weeks to pick up any other mail. This next period of my life promises to be intense and quite rewarding.

I did hear from Mary and Marjorie while I was in E. Grinstead. Please say thank you to them and tell them how much I appreciated their news. Thank God Philip is on the mend. I wish I had more time to write to each of my brothers and sisters individually. I rely on you to pass on items of interest. You must be writing every day just to keep up to all of us. I hope everything is good at home, including your very dear selves. My daily prayer is for you to be happy and contented. Love to all, *Jack* (Keefer, *Grounded in Eire*)

Dear Jack, March 7, 1944

I wish I were your age and could join you in this historic battle. What a privilege it will be to defeat the number one enemy of the world! I am supposed to be a humble clergyman but I confess pride in my three boys for their contribution to the coming victory.

Congratulations on your promotion to the Pathfinder unit. I understand they are quite an elite group of fliers and this is an honour for you.[ix] It is a daunting task that you are accepting but I believe you are up for the challenge. I know you have yearned to get back in the fight and now you have your chance.

The HMCS Owen Sound and its crew are doing us proud. They played an integral role in the sinking of a German U-boat that was full of supplies and ammunition headed for smaller submarines near the Bay of Biscay. They also sank two other submarines. I feel a connection as I followed the course of her development and attended the launch of her maiden voyage.

In sports, the Detroit Red Wings defeated the Boston Bruins to win the Stanley Cup in four games. It was quite one-sided but Judge Morley and I still wore ourselves out cheering and shouting at the radio. Of course we really wanted the Toronto Maple Leafs to be in the playoffs but it was not to be. Some may say that it's only a game but there's a lot of money at stake so I call it big business. I know you're on my side in that debate!

The World Series was won by the New York Yankees over the St. Louis Cardinals. Joe McCarthy is bowing out as manager and that will be a huge change for them. My favourite player, Joe DiMaggio, signed up for the war so he did not play this season. All in all it was a disappointing series, very low key. Did you happen to see the highlight film that was created as a gift for the troops overseas? Probably that would be worthwhile, just the exciting parts. However, the tension would be missing. Waiting for something to happen in baseball is half the drama. (I think I'll use that analogy in a sermon!)

Everyone on this side of the pond is expecting the final collapse of the Nazi regime this year. We have held our breath since 1939 and now we can smell the end of our fear. I realize that the final push will be tough and you'll be working steadily. Your mother and I intercede every night for you and your brothers, knowing that you are strong in your faith but might not have time for prayers.

I'll sign off for now, my dear boy. I am very proud of you. Enjoy being high in the sky again. See if you can touch the stars and say hello to our Gerald. Love, *Dad*

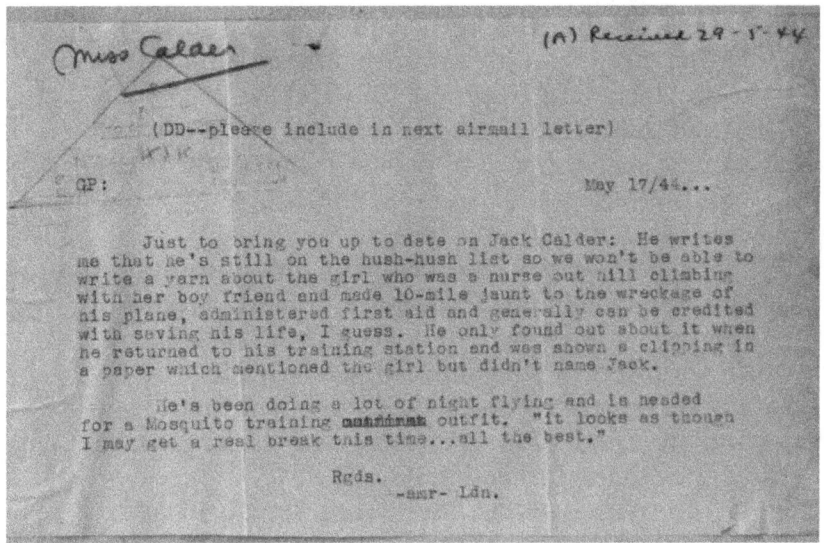

My Darling Jack, May 20, 1944

I am thinking of you always. Today the news was spread abroad by the *Manchester Guardian* and I don't know if you have heard through the channels of the RAF. I'm afraid it's bad news, so if you haven't heard, dear, please don't read this letter until you return from ops tonight. I want you to be fully alert to whatever task you must accomplish and not risk letting your mind wander to events that are over and can't be helped. I wouldn't be telling you, except that you might want to know the exact words of the announcement.

Sir Anthony Eden, Secretary of State for Foreign Affairs, yesterday rose in the House to announce the following, here's the clipping:

> I deeply regret to have to tell the House that His Majesty's Government have received information from the Protecting Power that 47 officers of the Royal Air Force, and Dominion and Allied Air Forces, have been shot by the Germans after a mass escape from Stalag Luft III.
>
> According to the information given to a representative of the Protecting Power by the

German authorities in the course of a routine visit to this camp on 17th April, 76 officers had escaped from Stalag Luft III on the 25th March.

Of these 76 officers 15 had been recaptured, 14 were still at large and 47 had been shot, some whilst resisting arrest and some in the course of a new attempt to escape after capture.

His Majesty's Government are profoundly shocked at this news and have urgently requested the Protecting Power to demand from the German Government a full and immediate report of the circumstances in which these men met their death and an explanation of its failure to report the facts at once to the Protecting Power.

The names of the officers shot were furnished to the representative of the Protecting Power on the occasion of his visit and the next-of-kin have been informed.

The House will wish me to express its deepest sympathy with the relatives and to pay tribute to the courage and high sense of military duty shown by all these gallant officers.[x]

We can rest assured that this is not the end of the affair. Fourteen officers, highly intelligent and trained fighting men are still at large and will have their wits about them. Also, we know that many civilians are sympathetic and hate the Nazis as much as we do, so the officers might find safe haven via the underground if they are lucky. The names of the deceased will likely be published in a day or two. Perhaps you know some of them.

All of us WAAFs are devastated by this news as it is clearly a breach of the Geneva Convention. The perpetrators will be brought to justice after the war, but today that is no consolation.

Still, my dearest, try to stay focussed on your work. Every day the mean-spirited on both sides use the war as an excuse to commit crimes. All we can do is fight for the day when justice will return.

I miss you, darling Jack. Love, *Ann*

Dear Mom and Dad, June 8, 1944

I can't tell you how much your letters mean to me. All the boys love to receive mail, of course, but not all have the warm, loving relationship that we have. I feel supported in every decision I make even when I hesitate to share some things with you. I hope life at home is ticking along well for you and that you're not sugar coating your news for my benefit.

I'll tell you a story of a storm at sea that affected our operation one night recently. The op was planned for a night bombing attack on gun emplacements at Calais, France. We left the ground and started across the Channel for the coast of France; however, it was soon apparent that a strong electrical storm was brewing. About halfway across the Channel the tips of the Browning machine guns began arcing static electricity between the barrels. An antenna trailing out about fifty feet behind the aircraft also was arcing electricity. The call came to abort the op, but worsening weather conditions forced a diversion to Upwood, a US base, instead of returning to Oakwood. Here we were briefed, given a full box of chocolate bars, and sleeping accommodations for the night. We flew back to Oakwood the following morning, unfortunately leaving early, without breakfast; however, they did give us large cans of juice.[xi]

Here's another unusual experience in the life of a flyer. The squadron was scheduled for a night op. We were briefed as usual and believed it to be a routine bombing mission. As we participated in three previous sorties since the 1st of June, there was no reason to suspect this trip was of any special significance. Our destination target was a German heavy gun emplacement at Merville, in Normandy, France. We departed the field in the late hours of June 5. We encountered light flak but no search lights or enemy fighters. We dropped our bombs and returned home six hours after lifting off, and only upon our return did we learn of the start of the D-Day invasion. One thousand and twelve aircraft took part in this attack on the coastal gun batteries of the Normandy coast, including forty-nine Mosquitoes,[xii] mine amongst them.

I may not have mentioned before the debt we owe to our ground crew who ensure the aircraft is in tip-top shape before each raid, and afterward do any necessary repairs. They boost morale by waving to us as we cruise down the runway, and greeting us when we return. Their hours are just as gruelling as ours and they receive few honours for their trouble, but we absolutely could not function without their dedication. Their expertise in inspecting the aircraft is crucial.

Lastly, Ann and I took a tour of Cambridge on one of our day-leaves. We visited The Eagle Pub, a famous watering hole for RAF and US airmen. Its mismatched chairs, burnished wood, aged brass, and worn ale pull-handles radiate warmth. In fact, the back room is known as the RAF bar. The most unique characteristic is the mottled amber ceiling, almost completely covered with graffiti. The boys stand on tables and use lighters, candles, and, in one case, a girlfriend's lipstick, to immortalize their squadron, plane, or initials onto the ceiling.[i] Oakington is not far from Cambridge so I could not resist visiting this seat of academia. Yes, we did walk around the university campus too. While I found it beautiful, it did not inspire me. Several men were scattered around wearing long black gowns — to what purpose I don't know. I prefer air force blue. The River Great Ouse is fine but we were not there at the time of the Oxford-Cambridge boat race.

We wandered into a quaint secondhand bookstore, a very dim and sombre place, where I came across *On the Art of Writing* by Sir Arthur Quiller-Couch, MA, fellow of Jesus College, King Edward VII Professor of English Literature/ Cambridge: at the University Press 1921. It is a collection of lectures delivered from 1913-14.[xiii] I find the whole cover plate, every detail, so curious. Would you ever find a book with items like "Jesus College," "King Edward VII Professor," "at the U Press" in Canada? Was Quiller-Couch knighted for teaching

Eng. Lit.? I purchased a copy from a small, thin man with a long, white ponytail. I can't wait to read it late one night by lamp light, sipping a glass of single-malt Scotch.

Ann is sitting with me, laughing at my romantic notions. She will mail this letter and sends you her very best wishes. Love to all, *Jack*

JACK CALDER AGAIN REPORTED MISSING AFTER OPERATIONS

Shot Down on Enemy Terrain

FLT. LIEUTENANT JACK CALDER IS AGAIN MISSING

Thoughts on the North Sea, the night of July 20, 1944

Flying home from Hamburg at 25,000 feet. The sky alive with explosives, the vibrant colours of anti-aircraft fire and searchlights. From out of nowhere a German fighter attacks our tail. I move into bombing position.

The plane burns. Smoke fills the air. Pungent smell stinks. Shots fired. I fall — betrayed by both legs. Pain seers my brain.

Dave is shouting. I'm lying across the door. He's kicking the escape hatch below me.

I tumble into the night sky and begin to freefall earthward. My stomach tingles. Adrenaline rush feels intense.

I see the coast of Denmark, the beach stretching forever. That same beach I was navigating moments earlier.

I'm a drifter in the lonesome sky.

I see the jagged white line of waves crashing onto the shore. Perhaps those waves will carry me to land. Perhaps.

Bunkers are hidden in the dunes. My nostrils sting with the sharp smell of cordite. My legs hurt.

Our aircraft spirals into the sea, the flame goes out. Good old Mosquito ML984.

Where is Dave's parachute? His silk should be visible from here. He wouldn't wait to evacuate.

Small whitewashed cottages line the headlands. Do the Danes see me silhouetted in the moonlight?

Time to deploy the parachute — pull the rip cord. Ouch, that familiar feeling of being sawn through. Thank god the girls packed my chute perfectly.

This is the part I love, drifting, sailing slowly. A silent breeze strokes my face.

We won the Battle of Normandy last month. Wing Co. congratulated us on prepping Juno for the attack of our ground forces.

What keeps the Germans fighting? When will they realize the war is over? Don't they long for home and peace?

The sea rushes to meet me. Prepare for landing. Feet first. Knees together. Arms protecting head.

Splash down.

Ah damn. Can't breathe.

Remember training. Concentrate. Slow breaths. Can't. Chest heaving. Out of control. Heart pounding, beating savagely. Brain buzzing. Thoughts scrambled. Don't panic. Body burning — skin exposed. Keep moving.

Parachute filling with water. Hurry — don't get tangled — detach myself — cut the lines.

Okay. Just in time. Down it goes.

Leg wounds feel cool relief. Hell — I'm not treading water properly. Gawd it's cold. Never mind. Turn over. Lie on my back … float ashore, quietly. If I arrive before morning, I can hide in the dunes until I figure out what to do. That might be difficult if my legs don't work. Hmm.

Plan B: Nice Danish lady walking dog discovers me, hides me in cottage. How? Husband has a wheelbarrow to carry me. What about the bunkers? Hmm.

Plan C: Nice Germans tired of fighting watch with amusement nice Danish couple rescuing me.

Mr. and Mrs. Dane dress my wounds which are much improved due to salt water bath. Neighbour in village is doctor who treats nice RAF flier to help war effort. Yes. Good plan.

I wonder where my sweetheart is tonight. Minsky's? She doesn't want to wait for the end of the war to marry. She is eager to marry soon. Are you pregnant, my darling?

I ache all over. My head hurts.

Which way are the waves rolling, towards land or out to sea? I thought I was closer.

Mom, are you and Dad sitting in the porch having a nightcap? Do you sense me thinking of you and home? Will the cosmos carry a message tonight?

It's a long way to Tipperary/It's a long way to go/ … to the sweetest girl I know … / Goodbye … /Farewell Leicester … /It's a long way … /But my heart's/ Right there. Yeah.

Brothers, are you safe in Italy? Are we watching the same stars tonight?

Come on, universe, kick in and save me one more time. Damn it's cold. Where's Dave? "Dave. Hey, Dave! Over here!"

A seal. Hello, Seal. What are you doing in my little patch of the North Sea? You're a nosy bugger. Curious, eh. Do you smell blood in the water, boy? Guess what? We've got company — a small shark. Go get him — that's it — swallow him whole. Lunch.

What about tomorrow? This adventure might not turn out as hoped. My brain feels fuzzy. Nurse, what happens next? How long do I have?

News flash on the wire: Incident message…

Focus. Report status: Hands froze. Sensation in arms-prickly. So much for swimming. I'll float home.

I'm being rocked in the cradle of the North Sea. Huge swells. Up — 2, 3, 4 — Down — 2, 3 — …. Comforting. Ironic.

Tired. Sleep, come…

Jack's Last Letters
(Authentic)

My Dear Marjorie: June 28, 1944

At long last, eh? I'm awful. But we have been working terribly hard lately and I'm in love with the new job. As you probably know, I've been transferred from beavies to new very fast stuff and I'm very excited about prospects — especially since the prospects are along diversified lines. And, as the boys say, "There's bags of future in it," because the aircraft are so fast and high-flying.

Tonight, I'm afraid, I'm a mass of scratches and bruises. It was only a bit of a bus crash, but everything seemed to fall on me. I don't need even so much as a stitch, but my eyes are going to be the oddest color. We were returning by bus from Cambridge, where we practised assimilated parachute jumps into water (a swimming pool) and climbing in and out of rubber dinghies. We had to jump from a ten foot board into the water in full flying kit. Great fun.

Ann is pretty wonderful. I wish I could see her more often, though. I know she is lonely sometimes. Her roommate, whose husband has just come back from Italy minus a leg, has moved out, of course. And she worries about her people, who haven't been getting all the sleep they might, because they live in the south of England.

I'm not writing an air letter to Mom immediately, because the supply is very low; so I wish you would pass on anything you consider worthy of passing on. And, don't worry too much about whether you get off one of your wonderful letters to me. Make sure, instead, that you write and phone regularly to Mom, because that's what counts most with me. Let her know that I am very happy in everything, except being separated from you people. Don't let her fear for me, because I'm not afraid and I'm heading for the job I have been trying to get back to for 2 ½ years.

Charlie Bruce says you're a real hit around CP. They all seem to think a great deal of you, and I'm certainly not surprised. It's really quite a good spot for you. I hope we shall be working together there before too many more months.

I haven't seen Phil yet but hope to before too long. There hasn't been a letter from Jake in a couple of weeks, either, but there'll be one along soon, because he's very good that way lately.

The Doc made me take this morning off to get over my crash. And tomorrow will be my first regular day off in ten days. So, I'm practically on a rest cure.

Love to all (and the best to GP), *Jack*

RAF Station
Wyton, Hunts
July 16, 1944

Mrs. A. C. Calder
St. George's Rectory
Owen Sound, Ontario

My Dear Mother:

Tomorrow Tommy and I push off to squadron on a station near Cambridge, a good station where we shall be well housed and fed.

So the long way back is ended now and I am happy to be into the thick of things again after the barbed wire and the hospital beds and the failure of my attempt to spend a little time with you. We shall be working very fast and hard, I expect, and our main interest outside of flying will be sleeping. There will be considerable leave, however, and I should be able to see a good deal more of these islands than I have seen already. I have been fortunate in that respect, haven't I?

But I've been fortunate in many other respects. I trotted down to a very pretty little church in the village this evening, and on my way back I thought of how I had been favored in the many little "incidents" which have occurred to me in my 3 ½ years away from home. I have just received a letter from Bobbie Armstrong, the girl who saved my life after the crash last summer. Apparently the RCAF finally is going to do something to recognize her because she was expecting the personal assistant to Air Marshal Breadner and asked me if I knew what he wanted. I do hope they do something worthwhile for her. And I hope you will write to her soon. She is Mrs. G. P. Armstrong, 55 Great Tattenhams, Epsom Downs, Surrey.

Well, I'm back, I'm back because I wanted to come back to it. I wasn't born to failure and disappointment. Quite a bit of me was broken up last time. But the realization of what is within us all wasn't broken, thank God. "For God hath not given us the spirit of fear, but of power, and of love, and of a sound mind."

Mom, a lot of the boys leave letters behind to be sent to their people if anything should happen to them. I never have written that sort of letter to you and never will. I feel quite strongly that I am not going to be killed; and because we shall be travelling much higher and faster than I ever have before, we should be "safer." But I don't want to preclude all possibilities and I know that you can be told these things now: That I am very happy; That if we should be attacked I am better informed and more alert than ever before about getting out of trouble; That if I should go "missing" I would want you to be very quiet about it — particularly when the newspapers phone — because I probably would be walking back to you. And if I should fail to get clear, I would want you to think of me as walking towards you anyway, for that is what I would want to be doing. There is no death, you know.

Love to all,

Jack

AIR MINISTRY
73–77 Oxford St., London, W.1.
13th July, 1945

Dear Mr. and Mrs. Calder,

I have been inquiring at headquarters for news of your son, Flight Lieutenant J. P. Calder. There is no word. Consequently, I am writing to share with you your son's final moments as mine was likely the last face he saw.

We were returning from a mission to Hamburg when suddenly Jack noticed we were being chased by a German fighter plane. We took evasive action but that guy held fast to our tail like a wasp sting. Ultimately the aircraft was hit by flak and Jack was wounded in both legs. He had moved into bombing position and was unable to reach the dinghy behind the seat he had just left. I gave the order to hit the silk as the aircraft was burning. Jack bailed out first wearing his Mae West.

I assume Jack ditched in the Elbe Estuary, closer to land than I was, as the aircraft was headed over the water. I came down in the sea about two miles from land where I spent the next six hours before being rescued by a German fishing boat. The fishermen took me to a POW camp where I was held until the war ended. Then I walked to the Channel and hitched a boat back to Britain.

Jack and I flew many missions together and I can assure you he was not only an able navigator but a fine chap, very likeable, easy-going yet intelligent and pragmatic when it came to his job.

Please accept my sincere sympathy. You have lost your son and no words of mine will serve to comfort you. However, know this: my last flight with Jack, I will never forget.

Yours sincerely,

D.L. (Dave) Thompson, Flight Lieutenant

R.C.A.F. Overseas

Excerpt from "A Wartime Log" by F/Lt D.L. Thompson, aged 23

It was a perfect summer's evening in Cambridgeshire when I took off in Mosquito B for Baker for what was to be my last operational sortie. (The time was 11.55 p.m., Thursday, 20th July, 1944)

Jack (my navigator/bomb aimer) and I had only arrived at Oakington a few days before, and this was our first trip together with 571 Squadron. Both of us had completed an operational tour. (For Pathfinders, a tour was 45 missions. For others, 30–35 missions.)

On this particular night the target for three squadrons of Mosquitoes was Hamburg. We were 'spoofing' for the 'heavies' — about 800 of them attacking an oil target in 'Happy Valley'.

Having previously attacked Hamburg on two nights in 1941, and knowing something of the Hun defences there, I was well aware that this was to be no easy trip, but I had every confidence in the aircraft I was flying.

Owing to a slight mechanical defect, we were late off, and, by the time we set course for Holland, we found that we were about twenty minutes behind the 'main force'. It was not very long before we were in trouble, and I was a little concerned when I found out that the oil pressure on the port engine was reading zero, and that the oil temperature was 'off the clock'. Much to my relief, however, after a quick check-up, I found that it was only the instruments that were defective.

By the time we had reached our first turning point, on the east side of the Zuider Zee, we had managed to make up five minutes of our lost time and we were confident that we could probably make up another five minutes or more before we reached the target. On this leg, however, we ran into more trouble — a German night-fighter! — and we wasted more precious time shaking him off.

We were now flying at 30,000 feet, and we intended bombing from 28,000 feet. When we were still 90 miles from the target we could see all the bombs exploding with vivid flashes on the ground, and the colourful markers and flares were cascading down. Flak and searchlight concentrations were very heavy and I must admit I was feeling a little nervous when I realised that we would have to go in alone. **Jack, who had now taken up his position at the bombsight, was as cool as a cucumber.**

Then came the bombing run. Large fires were burning and we had no difficulty in finding the target. Jack gave instructions over the intercom.

"Right, right …… steady …… left, left, steady …… steady …… bomb gone!"

We were carrying a famous 4,000 lb 'Cookie' and I personally gave a big sigh when the aircraft lurched and I knew that the bomb was tumbling down to earth.

No sooner had the thought passed through my mind when the aircraft lurched violently again. I was thrown out of my seat and hit my head on the roof, and I had some difficulty in steadying the aircraft. We had received a direct hit from heavy flak.

Jack was lying still in the nose of the aircraft and I knew he was badly wounded — I had been fortunate and received only a slight scar from shrapnel.

It would be impossible to remember exactly what took place in the next few minutes. My first concern was to get out of the searchlights and flak — the starboard motor had stopped, and there was a large hole in the nose of the aircraft. After a few seconds the starboard engine burst into flames and I tried in vain to put the fire out. It wasn't very long before the whole of the wing was on fire and there was nothing to do but abandon aircraft. Our troubles weren't over — the escape hatch had jammed, and, as Jack was unable to release it, I had to leave the controls and kick the hatch away. As Jack was lying over the escape hatch he was able to clip his parachute on and slide out. That was the last I saw of Jack and I'm grieved to learn now that he must be presumed killed.

I followed Jack out, leaving our burning aircraft at about 20,000 feet. I delayed my drop for a few seconds because of the height and I reckon I opened my 'chute at about 12,000 feet. The drone of B for Baker grew fainter and fainter, and a little while later I saw a vivid flash on the ground — the end of a very gallant aircraft!

Below me was a thin layer of cloud and I was unable to get any idea where I was going to land. At about 1,000 feet, I floated gently through a layer of stratus cloud and got a nasty shock when I could plainly see the coastline several miles away. I was in for a good ducking!

Splash! How far I went under I don't know, but I was soon on top again, kicking my parachute clear. Once I had freed myself I wasn't long in getting my dinghy in operation and, after a lot of puffing and blowing (I was just about out of breath by now), I dragged myself into it. It was just 2 a.m. (I knew that because my watch stopped as soon as I hit the water), and I was a long way from home.

In the distance the sirens were sounding the 'all clear'. A lighthouse at the entrance to the Kiel Canal commenced to blink its light again, and, one by one, the searchlights began to disappear.

I commenced to paddle!

Unfortunately I was a little too far from England, so I decided to try and make for the north side of the Kiel Canal. If I could get to shore before dawn I had a chance of escape. Well, either the tide was going out, or else the wind was blowing in the wrong direction, because at dawn I was still as far from the shore as when I commenced. Shipping began to appear all around me as it became light and I knew it wouldn't be long before I was spotted. A fisherman found me and took me aboard. He was very decent to me and took me to his house. I was offered a drink of coffee.

Soon afterwards two decrepit old men appeared with rifles at the ready — the Wehrmacht !! I was a POW. They took me along to their camp, where I was under guard until the Luftwaffe Officers arrived. I was searched and then, still wet through, taken to the railway station by car at Brunsbüttel, a town in northern Germany. Whilst waiting for the train, the air raid sirens sounded, and I was taken in a shelter. The natives were somewhat hostile!! That day I was taken to Hamburg (the city I had been bombing) and, on passing through, I was the cause of much excitement and quite a few of the population tried to 'get at me'. My guard kept them at their distance at the point of a revolver.

That night I spent a rather uncomfortable night in Hamburg Prison. I was there until 5 o'clock on the next day. I was then taken overnight to Frankfurt am Main, arriving there for interrogation early Sunday morning. For the next eight days I was in solitary confinement — then a quick journey to a transit camp at Wetzlar and the next day, along with some fellow countrymen and Armenians, I started on a four day journey to Barth.

(F/Lt D.L. Thompson arrived at Stalag Luft 1 on Friday, July 28, 1944 and stayed there as a POW until April 30, 1945 — his 24th birthday — when the Germans left the camp at midnight, having been defeated. The Russian forces arrived the next day, May 1, to liberate the men. That night there was a radio newsflash announcing that Hitler was dead!)

Pictures are taken from his Wartime Log book

AFTERWORD

Ann Mitchell and Bobby Keefer, supported by a circle of friends, waited at the Brevet Club for Jack to return on the night of July 20, 1944. When he did not show up, they kept watch for weeks, hoping for news that he had been taken as a POW. No word came.

In mid-September Bobby Keefer and a friend were having a drink, again in the Brevet Club, when their squadron leader, Grant Fleming, failed to return from a flight over Munich. They learned later that his Mosquito had been chased by one of the new, fast Messerschmitts. Fleming sent an SOS from his Mosquito at 35,000 feet before crashing in the Swiss Alps. His body was never recovered.

After Jack was shot in both legs and his Mosquito caught fire, he bailed out and drowned in the Elbe Estuary, west of Hamburg, near Brunsbuttel, in the North Sea. Six weeks later his body was found washed ashore by a German fishing boat. He was interred permanently in the British Military Cemetery in Kiel.

Most of the former POWs from the Curragh Camp died when they returned to operations. Bobby Keefer, Bruce Girdlestone, Aubrey Richard Covington, Chuck Brady, and Bud Wolfe survived and met for at least two reunions.

Ann Mitchell was devastated by Jack's death, but eventually recovered, as Jack would have hoped. Tragically she herself died in a hunting accident in 1952 (Keefer, 258–61).

Mary Kelly remained heartbroken over Grant Fleming's death. She never married.

In August, 1944, a memorial softball game was held in Chatham in Jack's honour. Donations resulted in a large trophy of a silver bowl, with baseball players on either side, and four plaques below for the winning teams in successive years. A central plaque shows Calder's name.

Flight Lieutenant Bobby Keefer retired from the RCAF and continued flying commercially.

Bruce Girdlestone served in the Pacific in 1944 and 1945 and became a successful architect in Christchurch, New Zealand.

Chuck Brady became a flight lieutenant and DFC winner and retired to Kelowna, BC.

Bud Wolfe retired from the US Army Air Corps as a Lt. Colonel and moved to Orlando, Florida.

Covington retired as a Wing Commander in the RAF.

Slapsy Maxie retired as a squadron leader.

Freddy Ball, Keefer's "Old Man," became Air Marshall Sir Alfred Ball, KCB, DSO, DFC.

Lieutenant Kelly, the guard at the Curragh who attacked Jack, became a judge of the Superior Court of Ireland.

Éire became the Republic of Ireland in 1949.

I Flew into Trouble

By FLYING OFFICER JACK CALDER, R.C.A.F.

(Article published by *Maclean's* magazine, August 15, 1942, after the manuscript was smuggled out of Curragh Prison by Jack's brother, Jake.)

Night raids on Naziland, high jinks at station H.Q., death-dodging in flak-torn skies — Canadian now interned in Éire tells of life in the bomber command

A hand fell on my shoulder and I turned away for a moment from the job of destroying maps, documents and instruments at the navigation desk. Keefer stood at my elbow, still carrying the hatchet with which he had chopped the rear gunner out of his jammed turret.

"I guess this means a long rest for us," he shouted. "I never thought we would end up in Ireland."

"Maybe we'll get out of it yet, Bob," I ventured, tongue in cheek. "We've been in tougher spots."

Keefer, captain of the aircraft, went forward and took over control from the second pilot. The wireless operator fired off another Verey signal cartridge, hoping to attract attention from some airdrome. I finished clearing my desk and went up beside Keefer to peer into the darkness.

"I always wanted to make a parachute jump anyway," he said over the phone.

"But not under these circumstances," I replied. "It's a long walk home."

For four months the two of us had been flying, rooming and eating every meal together. In those four months, attached to a Royal Air Force squadron in England, we had attacked shipping and inland targets from Brest to Bremen, from Boulogne to Berlin. Now we were running out of fuel over the west coast of neutral Éire on a chilly morning. Seeing that we couldn't reach Northern Ireland or England, Keefer had picked out a hole in the thick layers of icing cloud and we were circling above it, so that when we jumped we would be sure of coming down on land.

"Check the petrol again, will you?" he asked.

"There's enough for about five more minutes."

"Okay," he ordered. "Line up the crew. You and I will jump as close together as possible. I'll yell at you in the air and we'll try to get out of the country together."

I shook hands with the four sergeants as I herded them to the escape hatch. The rear gunner, who was on his first operation, was bleeding a little about the face. He said he was all right.

The starboard engine cut out. The front gunner kicked open the escape hatch on the captain's order and dropped through. The second pilot, rear gunner and wireless operator followed.

Jumping was easy. As my feet went out, the slipstream caught them and I was speeded through by the rush of air. I pulled the rip cord; in a moment my head was jerked back as the chute opened and I felt as if I were being sawn through. The sensation ended quickly and the first thing I noticed was the desperate quiet after eight hours of listening to the buzz of the engines and the crackling of the telephone.

I shouted for Keefer and got no reply. Then I heard the low whirr of our aircraft — old "C for Charlie" — gliding to her finish. Bob had planned to head her out to sea, but now she seemed to be coming around. I learned later that Keefer had headed her for the sea, started to jump and then had seen she was turning inland. He returned to the controls, pointed the machine for the Atlantic and jumped. The aircraft came around again and finally broke her back in a pasture.

Down in a Bog

For a long time I seemed not to be falling at all, just swaying a little in the breeze. I turned around to make sure that I wouldn't be carried out to sea and I inflated my "Mae West" just in case. Suddenly I realized the ground was near and I relaxed for the impact. Nothing happened. I bent my knees. My feet hit the ground and my knees hit my chin.

I got up, released my chute and tucked the folds under my arm. In the darkness I could see absolutely nothing but the stars and a couple of lights on the coast. I decided to start north and try to find Keefer. I stepped out smartly and immediately went to my hips in water. I retraced my steps and headed south; this time I sank to my knees in ooze and goo. Attempts west and east brought the same results.

It dawned on me that I was in a bog. It really wasn't a bad bog as Irish bogs go, but I was stuck there until dawn. I sat down on my little dry spot and ate a bit of chocolate, wondering all the while how the rest of the crew were faring. My head ached.

As the first light of dawn flooded the bog a half-hour later, I discerned in the distance what I thought to be a great wall. The light grew and, just about twenty yards from me, I picked out a ribbon of road. If I could have got to that in the darkness, I might have stumbled to some sort of hiding place.

Now I hid my parachute, waded to the roadway and fairly ran along it toward the wall, for there wasn't a sign of other cover. As I got quite close to the wall, however, I saw that it was made of piled-up blocks of peat, the winter's fuel supply for hundreds of Irish families.

I hurried past and came upon a gate bearing a sign: "Keep Gate Shut." The thought came to me: "Well, we speak the same language. Maybe they'll listen to an argument if they catch me."

Deciding to head for the coast, I tore the badges and insignia from my flying dress as I walked. Around me were the tiny white cottages of the turf-cutters, each with a noisy dog. Smoke curled above the thatched roofs.

The sun started to rise and, in desperation, I looked for a hiding place. A small copse close to a cottage seemed the most likely, and furtively I climbed the low stone wall to go to it. As I did so, a child came from the house.

"O momma," she cried. "Lookit the man!"

The family came out and I hurried away, wondering whether I was lucky enough to resemble and Irish vagrant.

The countryside was astir by now. Cattle drovers and donkey carts were on the road. Along the way I said good morning cheerfully to everyone. Dan O'Fagan said good morning from his pub door and the children sang good morning from the fence posts.

"Not bad," I thought, wondering if my red hair made me look like a native. "It can't be more than a hundred miles to the border, either."

When I had walked eight or ten miles I sighted a railroad track and then a patch of woods overlooking it, near a coastal village. It looked like an ideal spot to wait for a freight train, and I started toward it.

"Hello," I was accosted from the roadside. "Where are ye goin' and where are ye after comin' from?"

"I'm from the south and I'm going north," I told the Irish policeman, just as if I were addressing a traffic cop back home.

"Well, them as goes north always comes into our guard barracks for a nice cup o' tay," he smiled. It was a real, nice, top-o'-the-mornin' smile, but I could feel him frisking me with his eyes for firearms. There was nothing for it but to go along.

"We heared ye wuz comin'," he said. "Five others like ye will be along in a twinkle." And then wistfully, "Sure an' ye're all just lads, too."

In the police barracks I was fed bacon and eggs and Irish whisky, which goes down like fire and hits bottom like a sledge hammer. Keefer and the English sergeants came along soon. Bob was limping because, in landing, he had revived a knee injury which he suffered when he played with McGill University's football team.

"I had to go to a cottage," he reported. "The people said they would smuggle me into the North. So, while I was eating their bacon and eggs, they got the cops. Hey, look! Don't touch that Irish whisky. They gave me a shot and I nearly went through the floor."

The stories of the sergeants were similar to our own. They were in good shape.

The police and militia, arriving by the dozen, questioned us from every angle. Bob and I lied variously (and obviously) that we had brought a hundred parachutists and dropped them all over Ireland; that we had been flying alone and didn't know who the sergeants were; and that we didn't think we should be kept in a police station when our mothers and fathers came from Ireland and had been greatly interested in the Gaelic revival in America and the police strike in Boston. Keefer's name was O'Keefer and mine Fitz-Calder.

(I have learned since to swear that I am descended from the ancient Kings of Ireland and came "home" deliberately.)

When we had found out that we were at Quilty, in county Clare, we got permission to go outside and lie in the sun, for it was chilly in the barracks. We hoped, of course, to be able to get away, but the numbers of troops outside dashed those hopes quickly.

Bombs on Rotterdam

A bright sun shone on the sea, which lay calm and blue in the rock-bound inlet a mile away. All about us the land was green and in the background lay purple mountains.

While scores of Irish country folk stood gaping at us, Keefer fell asleep and I fell to thinking. I thought of the jobs we'd done and the fun we'd had together. Though I had been awake for more than twenty-four hours, I couldn't sleep. The letdown had been too sudden.

I remembered the tingling excitements of my first trip. It was to Rotterdam, where I released my first load of big bombs in the dock area. I was flying that night with Slapsy Maxie, a New Zealander who had been through the business in France and had flown the Atlantic twice. While he took avoiding action, he explained the various kinds of tracer shells that were being fired at us and the systems of searchlight fingers that were trying to pick us out, as if he were giving a lecture back in the crew room.

When we went to Frankfurt a couple of nights later, we were bounced around a bit by heavy anti-aircraft fire near Brussels; Maxie laughed while he worked the throttles to desynchronize the motors. On we went to find a terrific wall of fire being thrown up in one sector at the target area.

"There's something funny here," said Maxie. "I think they want us to believe the target is where they're shooting from. But do you see that bend in the river down there? That's what we're looking for."

When I dropped a flare, Maxie's opinion was confirmed. We were able to let the load go quickly and go back to England, where we were diverted to another airdrome because our own was under fog.

I did Brest in daylight with Maxie. It seems to have been the most exciting episode of my life, for our formation shot down three Messerschmitt 109s in our run-up to the target. Maxie got the Distinguished Flying Medal for that one.

Many of the jaunts with Keefer were nearly as successful. We couldn't have hit the target more squarely than we did on our first together. We just glided into Boulogne with a full moon ahead, released our stick across the docks and glided out again before Jerry knew we were there. The Air Ministry has recorded that the fires were burning the next day.

The things that stood out most prominently, though — as I lay on the green, green Irish lawn and gazed into the blue, blue Irish sky — were the things that had gone wrong and become right again, the things we had gone through and lived to tell about.

More vividly still I remember one night we headed for Berlin. An hour from the target — and after we had weathered a storm of anti-aircraft fire among the big searchlight belts — the wireless operator produced a message recalling us to base because fog was closing in all over England.

"Aw, we've gone through the worst of it now," Keefer groaned. "I feel like going on."

"But I've acknowledged the message, sir," the wireless operator said. "And my set is kicking up a fuss."

We would have to return, we agreed. Bob asked for a course for home and told me to select a target en route. We decided on an airdrome near Münster and I prepared the camera for our bomb explosions.

Sgt. Johnny Tett, the former Canadian diving champion, was with us as second pilot. One of his duties was to release the flash bomb for the photograph and he put it into the chute as we glided toward the target.

"Okay, Johnny?" I asked on the phone,

"Just about," he said; and then, "Holy smoke, no!"

There was a commotion and a flash lit up the aircraft and the sky around us. My first thought was of a night fighter or a new weapon. Johnny came on again.

"The thing fused too quickly," he panted. "It nearly went off in the aircraft. I think it exploded right beneath us."

We came around again, dropped our stuff and took a picture. We saw our fires for a good fifteen minutes on the way home. Johnny didn't say a word all the way.

As we approached England, we were diverted to a high-level airdrome, because our own was fog-bound. It took us a few minutes to find the place in the gathering mists. Then the most brilliant flare-path I had ever seen showed up.

"Broadway," I suggested.

"Yeh," Bob answered. "And, by the way, are you going to let me take down my hair and go to Minsky's tonight, or do we have to go the Rainbow Room again?"

But we spent the rest of the night sleeping on the floor in the officers' mess. So many aircraft had been diverted there that there weren't enough beds to go around.

When I awoke, whom should I find sleeping next to me but Stage-Door Johnny Allen, from our own squadron. We flew home in formation with him when the fog lifted, and 'shot up' our station with a low-level attack, contrary to regulations. When we landed, we found that the squadron had suffered the most disastrous night in its history. We went unpunished for our folly.

Movie Stuff

A few days later three new crews arrived to replace those we had lost. It was a cold, clammy morning and fog hung like a pall over the airdrome. The crews lolled about, cleaning guns and studying intelligence reports and photographs.

In the headquarters block was an empty office next door to that of our flight commander, who happened to be absent. The idea was conceived that I should sit in the empty office behind a desk and interview the new crews. Since I was wearing a raincoat there was no way of determining my rank and, for all the newcomers knew, I might have been something sacred like a wing commander. Keefer, dressed similarly, decided to pose as a medical officer. A flight lieutenant, who shall be nameless, offered to come dashing in spasmodically, saluting his 'senior officer' and bearing wild messages.

The new men were paraded in singly by an aircraftman with a perfect poker face. While the old hands rolled on the floor in mirth in the adjoining room, these innocents answered questions about whether they enjoyed going out with girls and how much liquor they could handle and still be fit for flying the following day. Dr. Keefer would conclude each interview with a frank discussion.

The flight lieutenant, who had seen "Dawn Patrol" four or five times, exercised a fine sense of the dramatic. He would burst into the room just when I was in the midst of a hushed statement on "death with honor."

"Ceiling is still zero and visibility a hundred feet," he would exclaim. "You can't send inexperienced crews up in this sort of stuff."

"I can't, eh?" I breathed. "The watchword on this squadron is 'keep 'em flying' and we can't let a little thing like fog stop us, particularly now that we've got the new fog-flying landing beam. It looks like an all-out effort on the big town tonight and those people are going to have to get used to the equipment before they go off."

The flight lieutenant would protest in vain, then go out muttering: "No wonder they call him the Killer."

Dr. Keefer just buried his face in his hands.

There was no flying that night, however, and the newcomers were treated to the joys of the "Passion Wagon," a bus which took the air crews to neighboring towns occasionally when operations were washed out. Laden with men bent on relaxing, it pulled out after tea and came back at midnight. In the meantime the townspeople watched mystified while the ice rink, the public houses and other entertainment centres bulged.

On one of our last raids we came home with three minutes petrol after visiting Bremen, Wilhelmshaven and Emden in search of a suitable target. Nowhere over Germany is the anti-aircraft fire more vivid than over the northwest; that night the whole countryside spurted fountains of varicolored shells.

The commanding officer was in a sweat when we arrived back an hour after everyone else, and his wife made us promise at dinner the next night that we wouldn't worry him again.

The flight on which we lost Coxie from the rear turret was a nightmare. We climbed to 20,000 feet over the North Sea, always just above a field of icing cloud. After crossing the Belgian coast, the machine suddenly gasped, went out of control and spiralled dizzily downward. Keefer brought her right after losing about three thousand feet.

Over the telephone I could hear Coxie shouting — though his voice came through like a whisper — to ask if everything was all right. I reassured him, and then the plane spiralled downward again. Bob wrestled her under control and finally the clouds divided as providentially as the Red Sea. We levelled out.

"We went into a cloud and iced up before I could do a thing," he shouted tersely. "I haven't any instruments left but my compass and altimeter. I'll have to go down below the freezing level."

We descended to three thousand feet. It was then we found that Coxie, unable to communicate with us and apparently certain that we were spinning in, had bailed out. We had lost the best rear gunner on the squadron, a boy who had three enemy aircraft to his credit and who never lost his spirit in the most nerve-racking spot in the ship. (He reports the food in a German prison camp "not so good.")

Our instruments gradually returned to normal and we bombed a coastal airdrome from so low a level that we felt our bomb-bursts. As we fought our way home across the North Sea in a thunderstorm, lightning struck the front guns with a flash that thoroughly scared us all and blinded the gunner momentarily. The white cliffs were never more welcome than on that night. On our last leave we had set a record by doing

Doncaster, Edinburgh, London and Southend in six days, seeing all the shows and meeting scores of friends from Canada. When we "left" our squadron, we were organizing a hockey team and we had just sold our £10 motor car for £15 because the license and insurance were due.

Once we had tea with the King and Queen and the Princesses in Windsor Castle. We chatted about the Royal Visit and the pre-war days.

Escape Frustrated

AND NOW we lay on a lawn in Éire, away from it all, waiting for a motor convoy to take us to the quiet of an internment camp. My headache grew worse.

In midafternoon the parish priest came to see us, saying that he was "sorry." Why I chose to unloose my feelings on him, I don't know; but I stood up and engaged him in the wildest political, religious and war argument on record. They say it was pretty good. It must have been, for I recall an old woman trying to collect sixpences in the crowd that looked on open-mouthed.

The convoy formed and we were driven down the coast and along the beautiful River Shannon to Limerick. That night we went behind barbed wire on the Curragh, where British troops were garrisoned in the last war. It was startling to see the streets lit up again at night, after Britain's blackout.

The Irish people? Well, they're very Irish. They've been very kind. We have been allowed considerable freedom on parole. John D. Kearney, the Canadian High Commissioner, has been like a father to us. Our parcels from Canada have been the envy of the entire British Internment Camp.

The atmosphere of horses, fishing and Irish colleens could be pretty lulling, I think. Somehow — and I believe the Irish understand too well — we aren't always thinking of those things. We can still read the papers and listen to Churchill and Roosevelt by radio.

The last escape attempt was a big one but got nowhere. Perhaps too many Irishmen know what it is to be locked up by other people. They've known all the tricks so far.

Republished courtesy of *Maclean's*.

Acknowledgments

A huge thank you to Ralph Keefer who ran before me telling Jack's story. Thank you for generosity in sharing the intimate details of Jack's life while in service and bringing him to life for me and my extended family; for allowing me to draw on his father's story-telling and repeat some of the tales told first in *Grounded in Eire* (McGill-Queen's University Press, 2001).

To Kathryn MacDonald for critiquing every letter with tough love; for countless conversations over meals; for glasses of wine on her boat, and inspiring me with her amazing poetry.

To Al Seyour and Tom Pickering, my partners in the prodigious historical writers' critique group of SOTH, whose keen eyes for detail kept me from embarrassing myself.

To Marie-Lynn Hammond for going out on a limb and pitching my story to Greg Ioannou at Iguana Books.

Thank you always to Terry Self for his kindness and patience showing me how to photograph each item in my grandmother's scrapbook, for gardening advice and country drives.

A big thank you to each of my beta readers: Donna Wagner, who not only read the ms but brought many more details to light as a result of her research skills; to cousin Jean McNeil for her perspective as an actor and her family knowledge; to Sue McNeil for reading and encouraging; to Carol Cooper Bustin and Byron Bustin for their effusive praise of the ms; to Mike Mason for his loving, in depth response as a fellow writer; to Karen Mason for her perception as a reader; to the lovely Deirdre Finnan for her insight into Irish ways.

Thank you to Felicity Sidnell Reid, Gwynn Scheltema, and Chris Cameron for repeated interviews on the Sunday radio program, Word on the Hills.

Thank you to Felicity Sidnell Reid, author of *Alone*, for conversations during nighttime rides from writing critique groups; for chairing the writers' group, Spirit of the Hills, which has been such a support and inspiration for years, for many cups of tea on her garden deck, and for poetry.

Thank you to Shane Joseph of Blue Denim Press for a spot on his webinar; for e-publishing my novel *Roadblock*; for publishing my stories in *Hill Spirits*, *Hill Spirits III*, and *Hill Spirits VI*; for technological help on other projects.

To *Maclean's* magazine for permission to republish Jack's article, "I Flew into Trouble," from August 15, 1943.

To Canadian Press for permission to reprint Jack's WWII newspaper articles.

To Professor Heidi Jacobs of Leddy Library, University of Windsor, for encouraging and collaborating with me on producing the website Jack Calder at War; for bringing to life Jack's sports writing of the 1930s in her book 1934: The Chatham Coloured All-Stars' Barrier-Breaking Year (Biblioasis, 2023).

To Sarah Glassford, University of Windsor, historian, archivist, and author of Canadian women's Second World War experiences, *Making the Best of It,* for seeing the historical value of my grandmother's scrapbook as a first-hand eye-witness account of World War II and for recognizing the imagined voices in Jack's story as authentic.

To Erin Monette and the team at the Canadian War Museum for accepting my grandmother's scrapbook into the collection because of its unique eye on the greatest war in which our country participated.

Thank you to the folks at Iguana Books, especially Cheryl Hawley, Lee Parpart, and Jonathan Relph for their expertise and patience in bringing *I Flew into Trouble* to its best level.

For Scott Chandler and his comic "All Stars: the true story of the 1934 Chatham Coloured All-Stars," featuring Jack's writing from his sports columns.

Thank you to John Lutman, Archivist, Diocese of Huron Archives, Huron University, London, ON for information concerning my grandfather, A.C. Calder and uncle, Gerald Calder, and the Bishop's charges during war years.

To Sherry J Pringle, author of *All the Ship's Men: HMCS Athabaskan's Untold Stories* (Lammi Publishing Inc. 2020), for her generous encouragement and information.

To Joanne Culley, author of *Love is in the Air* (FriesenPress, 2013) for her story and for sharing her experience with me.

To Bill Conall for stories and songs that inspire.

To Matthew Corrigan for believing in me from the beginning.

To Doug Robinson and Andrew Down and the team at Veritable Wealth Advisory who take such good care of money matters for me.

Heartfelt thanks to Linda Engel & Sue Kingwell who know the meaning of friendship and for always being available to listen; to the BCI gang and birthday girls and book club for laughter and stories; to Ruth White for lazy afternoons in the hot tub.

To Matt for faithful phone calls every week, for all kinds of help, and music; and Marta for regular doses of encouragement, books, and knowledge of all kinds. To both for understanding and unfailing love and those late-night talks by the fireside.

To Aviva, Danika, Rowan, and Cole, for sharing, laughter and music: the hope of the future.

Endnotes

[i] Ralph Keefer, *Grounded in Eire* (Kingston: McGill-Queen's University Press, 2001), 76. All subsequent references to Keefer's book will be given in parentheses within the text.

[ii] *The Globe and Mail*, 23 March, 1937, 19.

[iii] Francis M. Carroll, "United States Armed Forces in Northern Ireland During World War II," *New Hibernia Review / Iris Éireannach Nua* (Ireland: University of St. Thomas Center for Irish Studies: 2008), 15–36.

[iv] Wikipedia, "Bombing of Dublin in WWII," Accessed Aug. 5, 2024, https://en.wikipedia.org/wiki/Bombing_of_Dublin_in_World_War_II.

[v] Clayton Kraby, Reasonable Theology website, "Original C.S. Lewis 'Mere Christianity' Broadcast," Accessed Aug. 5, 2024, https://reasonabletheology.org/original-cs-lewis-mere-christianity-broadcast/. See also: Bruce R. Johnson, "The Efforts of C.S. Lewis to Aid British Prisoners of War During World War II," *The C.S. Lewis Journal*, Vol. 12 (Scheinsucht: 2018): 41–75.

[vi] Jack E. Thompson, DFC, *Bomber Crew*, 2nd ed. (Victoria, BC: Trafford Publishing, 2005), 13–14.

vii Kenneth B. Cothliff, *Four Who Dared, Inspiring Stories of Canadian Airmen in the Second World War* (Victoria, BC: Heritage House Publishing Company Ltd. 2019), 62.

viii Milton, John, "Sonnet 19: When I consider how my light is spent," PoetryFoundation.org, Accessed July 30, 2024, https://www.poetryfoundation.org/poems/44750/sonnet-19-when-i-consider-how-my-light-is-spent.

ix Jack's July 1944 letter to sister Marjorie mentions his new promotion: "from beavies to new very fast stuff." Also: all correspondence after August 1943 from RCAF and the Air Ministry at London, England to Jack's parents refers to Flight Lieutenant John Philip Sargent Calder.

x 392nd Bomb Group, "STALAG LUFT 3 THE GREAT ESCAPE," (1944). Also: Hansard, "OFFICER PRISONERS OF WAR, GERMANY (SHOOTING)," HC Deb, 19 May, 1944, vol 400, cc 437–9.

xi Bruce E. Hubley, *Pathfinder: The WWII Experiences of RCAF Air-gunner FO Russell F. Hubley DFC, CD* (Florida, USA: BookLocker.com Inc., 2013), 58–59.

xii Hubley, *Pathfinder,* 59.

xiii James M. Fenelon, "Time Travel: Yanks in Cambridge," Historynet, Feb. 17, 2017, Accessed Aug. 5, 2024, https://www.historynet.com/time-travel-yanks-in-cambridge.htm.

Bibliography

I have divided the sources into four parts. **First** are the original sources to which I am most indebted: my grandmother's WWII scrapbook including Uncle Jack's articles about Republican Ireland; Uncle Jack's articles published in *Maclean's* and *The Canadian*; and Ralph Keefer's book, *Grounded in Eire*. These sources I paraphrased and quoted freely, with permission.

Calder, Patricia and Jacobs, Heidi L.M. *Jack Calder at War: A Canadian Mother's WWII Scrapbook.* https://collections.uwindsor.ca/omeka-s/jack-calder-at-war. University of Windsor, 2023.

Calder, Ft. Lieut. Jack. "East Grinstead, Queen Victoria Hospital Canadian Wing." *The Canadian*, 1943.

Calder, Jack. "I Flew into Trouble." *Maclean's*, 15 August, 1942: 11, 25–27.

Keefer, Ralph. *Grounded in Eire*. Kingston: McGill-Queen's University Press, 2001.

Second are the sources I relied upon heavily for accuracy.

Cothliff, Kenneth B. *Four Who Dared: Inspiring Stories of Canadian Airmen in the Second World War.* Vancouver: Heritage, 2015.

Gibson, Guy. *Enemy Coast Ahead: The Illustrated Memoir of Dambuster Guy Gibson*. Barnsley, S. Yorkshire,

England: Greenhill Books in association with the RAF Museum, c/o Pen & Sword Books, Ltd., 2019.

Hubley, Bruce E. *Pathfinder: The WWII Experiences of RCAF Air-gunner FO Russell F. Hubley DFC, CD.* Florida, USA: BookLocker.com Inc., 2013.

Kagan, Neil and Hyslop, Stephen G. *Atlas of World War II: History's Greatest Conflict Revealed through Rare Wartime Maps and New Cartography.* Washington, DC: National Geographic, 2018.

Middlebrook, Martin and Everitt, Chris. *The Bomber Command War Diaries, An Operational Reference Book, 1939–1945.* Pennsylvania: Pen & Sword Books Ltd., 2019.

Simpson, Geoff. *Guy Gibson, Dambuster.* Barnsley, South Yorkshire, England: Pen & Sword Aviation, 2013.

Thompson, Jack E. DFC. *Bomber Crew.* Second Edition. Victoria, BC: Trafford Publishing, 2005.

Third are other books I referenced for setting and the language of the times.

Alexander, Eileen. *Love in the Blitz: The Long-Lost Letters of a Brilliant Young Woman to Her Beloved on the Front.* New York: Harper Collins Publishers, 2020.

Axelrod, Alan, ed. *Victory: World War II in Real Time.* New York: The Associated Press, 2020.

Bowyer, Chaz, Arthur Reed, and Roland Beamont. *Mosquito, Typhoon, Tempest at War.* London: The Promotional Reprint Company Ltd., 1997.

Carroll, Francis M. "United States Armed Forces in Northern Ireland During World War II." *New*

Hibernia Review/Iris Éireannach Nua. Ireland: University of St. Thomas Center for Irish Studies: 2008: 15–36.

Chandler, Scott. "Jack Calder Was a Man with a Story." Chatham-Kent Sports Network, June 10, 2021. Accessed Aug. 7, 2024. https://bit.ly/4dui8Lq.

Chant, Chris. *Allied Fighters 1939–45: The Essential Aircraft Identification Guide.* London: Amber Books, 2008.

Culley, Joanne. *Love in the Air: Second World War Letters.* Altona, MB: FriesenPress, 2013.

Gann, Ernest K. *Fate is the Hunter: A Pilot's Memoir.* Toronto: Simon & Schuster, 1961.

Gilbert, Lisa, ed. *Chatham Collegiate Institute Centennial History Book: 1885–1985.* Compiled by History Book Committee.

Gladwell, Malcolm. *The Bomber Mafia.* New York: Little Brown and Company, 2021.

Howarth, David. *The Shetland Bus: A WWII Epic of Courage, Endurance, and Survival.* Guilford, Connecticut: Lyons Press, 2018.

Johnson, Bruce R. "The Efforts of C.S. Lewis to Aid British Prisoners of War During World War II." *The C.S. Lewis Journal,* Vol. 12 (Scheinsucht: 2018): 41-75.

"The Last Voices of World War II: 75 years after the end of history's deadliest war, survivors share their stories." *National Geographic,* Vol. 237, No. 6. June, 2020.

Mitic, Jody, ed. *Everyday Heroes: Inspirational Stories from Men and Women in the Canadian Armed Forces.* Toronto: Simon & Schuster, 2017.

Quinn, Kate. *The Alice Network*. New York: Harper Collins, 2017.

Thompson, J. Stephen. *Lincoln Cathedral*. Victoria, BC: FriesenPress, 2018.

Fourth are the online references:

BBC (Archived pages). "WWII People's War: An Archive of World War Two Memories — written by the public, gathered by the BBC." Accessed May 11, 2022. bbc.co.uk/history/ww2peopleswar/ and WW2 People's War/ WRNS.

Canadian War Museum. "Canadian Newspapers and the Second World War." Accessed July 26, 2024. https://www.warmuseum.ca/cwm/exhibitions/newspapers/intro_e.html.

East Grinstead Museum. "Guinea Pig Club: Rebuilding Bodies and Souls." Accessed July 26, 2024. https://www.eastgrinsteadmuseum.org.uk/guinea-pig-club/.

Fenelon, James M. "Time Travel: Yanks in Cambridge," Historynet. Feb. 17, 2017. Accessed Aug. 5, 2024. https://www.historynet.com/time-travel-yanks-in-cambridge.htm.

Fusehill War Hospital: Carlisle. n.d. https://www.tulliehouse.co.uk/fusehill-war-hospital.

Mitchell, Chris. "Send Her My Love: Letters from World War II." CBN News, 2011. https://www.cbn.com/special/WW2letters/index.aspx.

RAF Wyton/ The Pathfinder Force. 1942–45.

Reading and Remembrance Project 2010. "Homeland Stories: Enemies Within." Accessed July 26, 2024. https://liberalstudiesguides.ca/wp-content/uploads/sites/2/2017/02/Reading-and-Remembrance-Homeland-Stories_Enemies-Within.pdf.

Washington Post. "Wartime Love Letters." Feb. 14, 2021. https://www.washingtonpost.com/history/2021/02/14/war-love-letters-valentines-day.

Wikipedia. "Archibald McIndoe." Accessed March 10, 2022. https://en.wikipedia.org/wiki/Archibald_McIndoe.

www.ingramcontent.com/pod-product-compliance
Lightning Source LLC
Chambersburg PA
CBHW032226080426
42735CB00008B/730